INTRODUCTION TO RECOVERY

A FACILITATOR'S GUIDE TO EFFECTIVE EARLY RECOVERY GROUPS

DEVELOPED BY

Michael Dean
501 Withdrawal Management Centre

with **Phil Lange**
Social Evaluation and Research Unit
Centre for Addiction and Mental Health

Centre for Addiction and Mental Health
Centre de toxicomanie et de santé mentale

A Pan American Health Organization /
World Health Organization Collaborating Centre

INTRODUCTION TO RECOVERY

A FACILITATOR'S GUIDE TO EFFECTIVE EARLY RECOVERY GROUPS

For information on other Centre for Addiction and Mental Health publications or to place an order, please contact:

Marketing and Sales Services

Centre for Addiction and Mental Health
33 Russell Street
Toronto, Ontario M5S 2S1
Canada
Tel.: 1 800 661-1111 or 416 595-6059 in Toronto
E-mail: marketing@camh.net
Website: www.camh.net

2173 / 06-04   P568

Acknowledgments

It is our pleasure to acknowledge the hard work of our staff team here at the Centre for Addiction and Mental Health's 501 Queen Street Withdrawal Management Centre. Team members — Sam Apostolou, Crystal Bell, Bill Carr, Wayne Charles, Paul Horrigan, Dolly Juanero, Stephen Layne, Nora Macdonald, Richard Mariapen, Patty Negashar, Ed Shinniman, Lori Slaunwhite, Tom Vosylius and Christine Werbski — were consistently patient, enthusiastic and constructively critical during the development of these group modules. Without them we would not have known whether the concept and modules were effective. Very special, heartfelt thanks are due to Jack Johnson, of Sault Ste. Marie, for his knowledge, trust and encouragement. In addition, we would like to acknowledge Trish Dekker, of the CAMH, for her help with the module on nutrition.

Thanks are also due to the following CAMH staff for their assistance in preparing this guide for publication: Nancy Leung, Myles Magner, Rhonda Mauricette and Patricia Drapeau.

We wish to dedicate this manual to the clients of 501 and all early-recovery environments. The challenge that faces each of these individuals is great, but working with many of them during the development of these modules assures us that they have the spirit and knowledge to succeed.

Michael Dean, ICADC
Service Manager, 501 Queen Street Withdrawal Management Centre
Centre for Addiction and Mental Health

Phil Lange, MA
Research Associate
Centre for Addiction and Mental Health

PREFACE

In November 1991, staff at the Addiction Research Foundation* Detox (also known as 501) began to facilitate informal group discussions with clients who were physically able to participate. The need for these groups was identified from a number of perspectives. First, detox staff noticed that after clients had completed the worst of their withdrawal, they often became anxious and bored. At this point they were in a state of "limbo" — they did not need constant monitoring for withdrawal, but were not emotionally prepared for discharge. Because they had too much free time with too little structure, they often engaged in conversations that glorified their drug use. Such "war stories" posed a barrier to clients recognizing that positive lifestyle changes were both needed and possible. Staff members believed that if clients' unstructured time and nega-tive conversation could be turned into a positive learning experience that promoted lifestyle changes, clients would then reflect on their detox stay as a positive experience.

From another perspective, the recently released *Report on the Operational Review of Ontario Detoxification Program* recommended that detox centres assume a more active role in discharge planning. We viewed this recommendation as an invitation to develop a systematic approach to discharge planning that included client education. Our approach addressed the following two areas: the need for positive conversation and the fact that clients needed general information to help them make informed lifestyle decisions. Our goal was to develop a series of psychoeducational groups that could be facilitated by one staff member. This approach would prove to be an effective and cost-efficient tool to promote recovery and discharge planning.

Experiences in other detox programs across the province supported our efforts. These centres facilitated "pre-treatment" groups that prepared clients for post-detox treatment. However, there was little structure within these groups, with the exception of showing videos and discussing the content. Furthermore, a rudimentary literature search found nothing on what to discuss or how to present information to clients in detox centres. Anecdotal evidence showed that people participating in group discussions in a detox prior to moving on to intense treatment needed less orientation time to the group component of the treatment program. This, in turn, led to clients spending more time on treatment issues. So, armed with our experience and that of other centres, we began facilitating Introduction to Recovery sessions. The name of the sessions reflects the fact that we wanted to get people thinking about recovery and introducing them to possibilities for lifestyle changes.

The years spent developing this group proved to be very worthwhile, for our clients repeatedly reported that the sessions were an important part of their stay in detox and in discharge planning. During this period, we screened many videos, trained staff in group facilitation, and renovated a vacant space into a group meeting room. We even tried psycho-drama in the sessions. Our experiences convinced us that a more formal approach to this project was needed for the next stage of development. In April 1997, we secured the help of a researcher to develop 10 education-based group modules. We hope that detox staff — and other professionals who work with people in early recovery — find these modules to be as valuable for their clients as they have been for clients at 501.

* The Addiction Research Foundation is now a division of the Centre for Addiction and Mental Health.

Table of Contents

Introduction

INTRODUCTION

What Is This Guide For?

The purpose of the Introduction to Recovery group is to exchange information that will help clients make informed lifestyle changes and orient them to the concept of "group" in preparation for ongoing treatment. *Introduction to Recovery: A Facilitator's Guide to Effective Early Recovery Groups* was designed to assist staff with the facilitation of such groups within withdrawal management and other early recovery settings. The group sessions are based on the concept of providing clients with as much information as possible in a short period of time. If the theory of a "window of opportunity" holds true, then providing as much information as possible may help sow the seeds of a fully blossomed recovery.

What Information Is Presented in Group Sessions?

These modules address a wide range of themes and issues that clients and detox staff have found to be both relevant and practical. The 10 modules address the following themes:

- the physiological aspect of addiction — "What is happening to my body now that I am not using/drinking?"
- inspirational, individual achievements — "How did other people overcome the problem?"
- community support — "What do I need in recovery?" and "How can I stick with the winners?"
- plans of action — "Whom do I speak with and where do I go from here?"
- general health issues — "What are the HIV and related risks, and lifestyle changes?"
- denial — "I am not sure I am as bad as other people" or "I am different from other people"
- pre-treatment — "I don't like group, yet I know that it is a part of treatment."

Who Can Benefit from the Group Experience at the Early Recovery Stage?

Although this guide was developed in the context of a withdrawal management centre, the information is relevant for any group of people in "early recovery." For example, group sessions can be held with:

- clients of agencies, both residential and non-residential, who are waiting to enter a formal treatment program
- clients who do not necessarily need formal treatment but can benefit from obtaining pertinent information
- clients who have already attended treatment and are currently in transition back into the community
- clients who are involved in treatment and could also benefit from this educational material.

These sessions are most effective for clients who are physically, emotionally and cognitively capable of participating; that is, they are not experiencing withdrawal symptoms that will detract from their experience. These sessions may not be appropriate for the following groups:

- clients who are distressed
- clients who need more attention and effort than usual
- clients with concurrent mental health disorders who may need to be stabilized on medication before attending group.

In cases where clients are incapable of participating in the group session, it is important to discuss the reasons why with them rather than simply excluding them from group sessions.

Who Should Facilitate the Groups?
What Qualifications Are Needed
in a Group Facilitator?

To a great extent, client participation and success in the group will depend on the facilitator's engagement skills. Our experience has shown that facilitators who used basic group skills, effective visual aids and appropriate engagement techniques had the greatest success with their groups. In general, this guide was designed for staff who have some experience working with clients in early recovery from substance abuse.

Although this is not an exhaustive list, this guide has proven useful to the following groups:

- graduates of community college human service counsellor programs
- staff with training in basic group theory or group facilitation
- staff with residential experience, who can incorporate information about individual group members (based on their stay thus far) into the group experience.

New or inexperienced staff should first co-facilitate a group a few times before facilitating independently. The goal is to bring what is known about the client into the group. For example, it is important to know whom to engage in order to increase their participation in the group and to recognize who is apprehensive of the group.

The facilitator's credibility will often influence how clients accept the presentation. Our experience shows that clients appreciate and relate to facilitators who:

- are caring, trustworthy and non-intimidating
- are not rigid about house rules
- are responsive to clients' often immediate needs by providing appropriate information, support and reassurance
- have a true understanding of the content of the material and who recognize what is important and what is not. In general, clients do not relate well to facilitators who only know about long-term and dangerous substance use from taking courses and reading.
- are in recovery themselves and talk frankly about what has helped or hindered their recovery
- can adapt the content (rewording text, making up their own examples) to meet the unique needs and interests of the group
- can effectively use overheads by showing them at the right time and can draw group members into discussion. Less skilful presenters just present the overhead without providing any introductory comments and simply expect the overhead to say it all. Effective presenters also show only a portion of the overhead to maintain interest and focus attention.
- stay focused on the module topic and keep the discussion focused with structure, control and direction. Good facilitators will break up crosstalk and end monologues. They will also leave aside their own personal agendas and present the material in the module.

Presenters who want to be more effective may benefit from the following hints:

- feel good about learning to lead better and better groups
- avoid the all-or-nothing view that other presenters have superior skills. Instead, recognize your own unique skills and gradually improve on each of them.
- feel a sense of your own worth as a presenter and of the clients as participants — not as rivals for control
- take pride in delivering the modules successfully — and in helping your clients!

Staff, as well as clients, can experience personal growth and gain self-esteem and insights from presenting these modules.

How to Use the Guide

What's Inside?

This guide comprises 10 psychoeducational modules, each of which takes approximately 90 minutes to present. The modules cover a wide range of topics and issues that are important to individuals in early recovery from substance abuse. Each module includes the following components:

- background information for the facilitator, including a checklist, presentation goals and objectives, and audiovisual requirements
- special considerations for dealing with each topic
- a list of group norms
- a presentation script
- worksheets that can be photocopied and used to engage client participation
- overheads

The guide also provides detailed descriptions of videos that can complement the presentations. Participant evaluation forms are also included, which provide facilitators with valuable feedback about their presentations. This information can be used to modify their approach to better meet client needs and become more effective presenters.

How Are the Modules Organized?

The modules were developed according to a 10-session cycle with topics following a natural order. However, the modules are also independent of each other, so you can choose whichever topic your group wants or needs to discuss. Depending on the client and the agency, some clients may be exposed to only one or a few of the modules, while others may be exposed to all of them. For example, if the group consists mainly of new clients, it may be helpful to begin with the continuing care module, even though that module may have been presented a few days earlier to a different group. If you work in a non-residential agency and do not know whom to expect before the group arrives, do a quick assessment of the group's needs and then choose the most appropriate module. A summary of the modules is provided in the next section of this guide.

In some cases, developing and incorporating a module specific to a target population will be helpful (i.e., a specific module related to women's issues would be appropriate for a female group). However, if a module is developed, the format should be consistent with the other modules. This will avoid confusion for the presenters.

Group Norms

In general, once clients in early recovery accept that they need assistance to recover, they appreciate a fairly directed and structured approach to treatment. Group norms provide one way in which to add structure to the group. At the start of each session, group norms remind participants of the basic rules of the group and common courtesy issues. There are two main factors to consider when deciding how the group will run: the purpose of the group and the expected participation level of group members. It is also important that the group sessions be at the same time and in the same place. Inform other staff members that group sessions are a priority. Encourage clients to attend external appointments at times other than at the group's time.

At the beginning of each session, restate both the main purpose of the group and the specific purpose for that day's session. This will help to orient new group members to the objectives of the group session.

Overheads/Worksheets

To maximize group participation, we reviewed various ways to better engage clients. Using overheads and a whiteboard can be the most effective way to present routine information.

This provides clients not only with visual aids, but also reinforces their participation and suggestions of ideas. Although videos can be a strong catalyst for discussion, they can sometimes allow participants to "doze off" while the lights are low or, if clients have already seen the video, they may use this as an excuse for not participating.

Videos

Appendix A lists a core group of videos that we have reviewed and consider to be appropriate for clients in early recovery. Other videos were not included because they were too long or had too narrow a focus.

In some cases we found that the videos were "triggers" for clients. Triggers are stimuli for negative behaviours associated with substance abuse; for example, a video on HIV education that demonstrated the correct and safe way to use a syringe was a trigger for our intravenous drug users. However, it is impossible to screen out all triggers and arguably it is best for clients to be exposed to some triggers in the supportive environment of the Introduction to Recovery group where they can practise effective coping skills. Once clients recognize and accept the support, the triggers will not be as threatening.

Group Discussion

One of the main purposes of the information presented in the modules is to promote positive and helpful dialogue between clients and staff. Clients place a high value on everyone in the group participating; groups are often rated higher or lower according to the number of people, and their willingness to participate. Remember that you do not have to cover all of the information in the module. As long as the dialogue is positive and related to the general topic, take the opportunity to engage in more spontaneous information-sharing. Sometimes the topic itself is enough of a catalyst for a productive discussion.

If there is no catalyst for interacting, however, discussions can take a negative tone, in which group members create reasons for not making positive lifestyle changes. If there is a lack of focus, you may be caught off guard by the negativity within the group. Only highly experienced group facilitators will escape such sessions unscathed.

Client Participation

Involve clients in the process. For example, asking them to help set up the overhead equipment will add validity to the information being presented. Also, participant evaluation forms give clients the opportunity to provide feedback on the content of the presentations. Group size will also influence the extent to which clients will participate.

When, Where and How Often Should the Group Be Held?

Holding the group sessions in the same room where clients watch television, play cards and eat their meals will diminish the importance of the group. If possible, select a comfortable secluded room that is separate from the main activity areas. Allow at least 90 minutes for the session. This allows time to discuss any general issues associated with the clients' stay before the actual session begins.

What to Expect in the Group

The dynamics of early recovery groups vary. During periods of high client turnover, group dynamics can change daily. For example, clients may hold back from participating in the group when new people join the group. Or, when the same clients meet every day, other group dynamics occur.

A particular challenge for staff and administrators are highly negative clients who recruit other clients to complain and even confront staff. A joy for clients and staff, however, occurs when an ongoing group achieves better rapport, and its members feel they are increasingly confronting the issues that will help their recovery, and simply feel closer to each other. This rapport may even lead clients to organize their own impromptu meetings outside of group time to discuss their recovery further.

What Do Clients Expect from Group?

Some groups will have a mix of clients whose motives may range from an absolute, burning conviction that they will gain their sobriety, to those who are clearly there for shelter, food and health reasons and who may say that they do not want to attempt sobriety. Many are interested only in information about their own preferred substance. A drinker, for example, may feel that his or her time is wasted because alcohol isn't the topic of discussion, and may even say that he or she doesn't want to hear about drugs.

Other clients may request more detailed information, including the effects of their preferred drug(s) on their systems, the diseases that could affect them, the good and poor foods for people in recovery, and the outside groups that they can access to help with their recovery. Many clients have accepted that their recovery depends on coming to understand the crucial missing element(s) in themselves or their emotional development. These clients are often the most enthusiastic participants in group, because they are confident that they will learn important new information.

Clients in withdrawal management centres may depend on the group session as a formal resource of information as well as an opportunity to share mutual ideas and plans. It can be very detrimental to clients' recovery if they are looking forward to the group and it is cancelled. As long as there is one appropriate participant, the session should take place.

How to Make This Guide Work for You and Your Clients

Place each module in the context of your agency and consider changing it to suit the unique needs of clients in your facility. Some of the modules will need to be adapted to your specific agency or milieu. For example, the module entitled "Withdrawal and the Next Step," though applicable to most withdrawal management centres, includes detailed procedural information that should be adapted or replaced to reflect the way your program or agency functions. In the case of clients who have recently attended treatment and are currently in transition back into the community, the issue of preparing for treatment will need to be revised, for a few of the modules discuss preparation for treatment. The general principle is to take what you need from the manual and build on it based on your own needs and expertise.

As you gain experience facilitating early recovery groups, and as you receive feedback from participants, you may become aware of other issues or develop ideas that would be helpful to other withdrawal management and early recovery groups. This information would be valuable to us and may lead to the development of additional modules that can be added to your manual in the future. We invite you to send us your comments using the questionnaire included in the evaluation section of this manual (see Appendix B).

Overview of the Modules

The following provides a brief summary of the 10 modules included in the guide:

Withdrawal and the Next Step provides practical information about withdrawal and is particularly relevant
to participants' current situation. Clients learn about their detoxification and withdrawal effects,
and the type of services that withdrawal centres provide. The specific objectives of this module are:

1. to teach basic biological processes of substance withdrawal
2. to relate detox activities to proven withdrawal management information
3. to demonstrate a logical flow from admission to discharge for each client.

Group promotes discussion and provides participants with insights about themselves. The specific objectives
of this module are:

1. to provide background information on the purpose of group sessions for clients in recovery
2. to promote client participation in group
3. to encourage and support clients sharing their positive experiences about this and other groups.

Early Recovery presents participants with insights into what is important to their future recovery.
The specific objectives of this module are:

1. to give background information on what has worked for others in early recovery
2. to encourage clients to prepare themselves for early recovery
3. to encourage and support sharing with others about early recovery
4. to understand the stages of recovery.

The 12 Steps is designed to help clarify the 12-step approach and promote it as a possible tool in recovery.
The specific objectives of this module are:

1. to provide background information on the 12 steps
2. to promote the 12 steps as a viable option for some of our clients
3. to encourage and support sharing at a 12-step level.

General Wellness provides clients with information on how they can increase their own wellness.
The specific objectives of this module are:

1. to encourage clients to seek the enjoyable feelings that are a part of wellness
2. to teach basic principles of wellness, especially around areas likely to affect people with addictions
3. to provide interesting new information on wellness — information that clients probably won't find
   elsewhere during early recovery.

Nutrition provides information on recovery-related habits in relation to nutrition.
The specific objectives of this module are:
1. to initiate an informal and supportive discussion of clients' food/nutritional preferences, providing reassurance that they won't be scolded, corrected or made to feel ashamed
2. to present some of the adverse effects of addiction on nutritional health
3. to present ways in which clients can improve their food choices.

Relaxation for Recovery offers insight on how relaxation can help clients deal with stresses that can lead to relapse. The specific objectives of this module are:
1. to provide background information on stress and relaxation techniques
2. to encourage clients to think of how relaxation exercises can help their recovery
3. to encourage and support sharing with others around this topic
4. to demonstrate the effectiveness of using audiotapes as a relaxation aid.

Spirituality covers the spiritual aspects of recovery. The specific objectives of this module are:
1. to provide information on the benefits of spiritual aspects of recovery
2. to promote participation in this module as a way of beginning to think about spirituality and how it relates to life in recovery
3. to encourage and support clients sharing their experiences, thoughts and attitudes about spirituality
4. to understand the differences between spirituality and religion.

Continuing Care gives clients information on the specific sources of help available to them.
The specific objectives of this module are:
1. to help clients begin thinking about how they will choose the types of services they will need to access
2. to help clients understand admission criteria for other programs
3. to encourage and support sharing with others around this topic.

Denial covers a topic that is important to client recovery and is a crucial factor in their addictions.
The specific objectives of this module are:
1. to define denial
2. to encourage and support sharing about denial and its role in the lives of users, as well as in the lives of people who don't have an addiction.

INTRODUCTION TO RECOVERY

Withdrawal and the Next Step

WITHDRAWAL AND
THE NEXT STEP

FACILITATOR'S CHECKLIST AND INFORMATION

Before you start, check that you have the following:

• overheads
1. Definitions
2. Approximate Time Frames for Detoxification
3. Symptoms of Withdrawal
4. Intake Phase — The First 24 to 48 Hours
5. Maintenance/Motivation Phase
6. Discharge Phase
• a copy of a withdrawal monitoring checklist

Audio/Visual Requirements

• overhead projector and projection screen
• whiteboard and marker

Purpose of the Module

to provide an overview of why and how we offer withdrawal management services

Objectives

1. to teach basic biological processes of substance withdrawal
2. to relate detox activities to proven withdrawal management information
3. to demonstrate a logical flow from admission to discharge for each client

Special Considerations

• Some clients have been in detox programs several times before without completing the withdrawal process, and may be resistant to participating in the group.
• Some clients may want to compare detox programs; these comparisons should be avoided.
• Throughout the session it is important to emphasize the unique nature of each client's experience.

NOTE: The facilitator's script and other material to be covered in the group session is in plain text. Instructions for facilitators are presented in **Bold** text.

Getting Started

Each time you start the group, review the following:

Group Norms

• Arrive on time.

• No food or drink is allowed during group sessions.

• Group members will sit in a semi-circle around the whiteboard.

• With the exception of washroom breaks, anyone who wishes to leave the group must first ask the facilitator's permission.

• Any feedback to other members is limited to how you relate to what has been said. Please do not give any advice or make judgmental comments.

• Only one person may speak at a time.

• Any other suggestions for today's group?   **Ask participants.**

How is everyone today?   **Ask around the circle.**

Does anyone have any issues that they wish to raise regarding the Detox Centre?

Introduction

The main purpose of the Introduction to Recovery Group is to exchange information that will help you make informed lifestyle changes and orient you to group in preparation for ongoing treatment.

The purpose of this session, Withdrawal and the Next Step, is to give you an overview of how we developed this program and why we believe detox is more than just a place to withdraw from substances.

The Session

Withdrawal involves certain changes to your body and mind — changes that happen to everyone. We will discuss some of these changes today.

These changes mean that during withdrawal the detox program needs to do certain things for your safety and comfort. We will discuss how some of our procedures are related to what happens to you during withdrawal.

But what happens after withdrawal? What do you do next with your life? We need to talk about motivation, and what you do while you are here and after you leave.

Generally, everybody's stay consists of three phases of care:
• Intake Phase
• Maintenance/Motivation Phase
• Assessment/Discharge Planning Phase.
We will discuss these in detail later. But first, I want to ask you why do you think people come to detox?

We will now try to show you what happens in withdrawal.

At this point go to the whiteboard and record some of the clients' responses. Possible responses could include the following: need referral to treatment; need emotional support; need a safe place to be; need a place to stay; need help to manage relapse; need a place to "dry out."

Show overhead 1 (Definitions) and explain that the following overheads are general statements and figures; each client's experience may be different. Attempt to solicit feedback about each overhead.

Show overhead 2 (Approximate Time Frames for Detoxification). If necessary, restate that these are general figures.

Show overhead 3 (Symptoms of Withdrawal), again stating that these are average symptoms and not everyone experiences all of them.

When staff checked on you while you were in the intake phase, they were looking for the symptoms we just discussed.

Hold up a withdrawal monitoring checklist (WMC) and briefly explain that the symptoms are on this sheet and staff use it as a reminder of what to look for. Prompt feedback from the group.

Now we will show you some overheads that will demonstrate how we make some decisions about your care. On these overheads, decisions are identified by diamonds and actions are identified by squares.

Show and discuss overhead 4 (Intake Phase).

Do you feel you are motivated to change your lifestyle? If not, what is missing?

Have you been motivated to change your lifestyle by something or someone since coming to detox?

Have you been approached by staff about helping you to develop a discharge plan? How many of you have a plan in place? Can one or two of you share your plans?

Are you aware of what your responsibilities are in your plan and what we will do on your behalf?

Wrap Up

Now, to summarize the session, we discussed what withdrawals are and then we compared some personal experiences. We talked about how some decisions are made in detox and what some of the processes are. We also discussed discharge planning. Before closing, does anyone have any other questions?

Thank you for participating in the group. Remember: no matter what your experience in detox is, it is up to you to follow up with your commitments to get all the benefits from your stay in detox.

Definitions

Detoxification

The process by which an individual is withdrawn from the effects of a psychoactive substance (World Health Organization 1994).

Withdrawal

The results or symptoms of detoxification.

Withdrawal Management (Detox Centre)

The assistance given during the detoxification process, and, if needed, additional support and treatment planning.

Approximate Time Frames for Detoxification

Notes

■ Time frames *do not* represent the entire detoxification process; i.e., symptoms may diminish but some substance still remains in your body.

■ Time frames depend on the quantity of substance, length of use, lifestyle and other social influences.

> alcohol: 3 to 5 days
>
> cocaine: 1 to 2 days
>
> heroin: 5 to 7 days
>
> benzodiazepines: dependent on many variables

Adapted from: U.S. Department of Health and Human Services (1995). Tip Series # 19.

Symptoms of Withdrawal

(These symptoms are not the same for everyone.)

Alcohol	Cocaine	Heroin	Benzodiazepines
anxiety	dysphoria (unhappiness)	anxiety	anxiety
restlessness		restlessness	muscle tension
insomnia	exhaustion	insomnia	insomnia
nausea and/or headache	sleepiness	nausea	psychosis (mental derangement)
	hunger	runny nose	
tremors	craving	sweating	abnormal brain activity
seizures	depression	goose bumps	
impaired concentration		irritability	seizures
		dilated pupils	
sensitivity to sound		yawning	
		cramps	
disorientation		spasms/aches	
hallucinations		diarrhea	
paranoia			
agitation			
diarrhea			
sweating			

Adapted from: U.S. Department of Health and Human Services (1995). Tip Series # 19.

Intake Phase – The First 24 to 48 Hours

■ You arrive at the centre intoxicated or in withdrawal or crisis.

■ You are assessed by a program worker.

■ You get into bed to recover from acute intoxication or withdrawal.

◇ When you are no longer intoxicated, you and your program worker decide if you are able to take a shower.

■ You take a shower and a program worker helps you change into comfortable clothes.

■ You are monitored by a program worker for 24 to 48 hours for acute distress, vomiting, breathing difficulties and level of intoxication/withdrawal.

◇ You and your program worker determine if you are ready for the maintenance stage of detox.

■ indicates an action taken by the program worker or the client.
◇ indicates a decision made by the program worker and the client.

Maintenance/Motivation Phase

◇ You and your program worker decide if you are able to attend the Introduction to Recovery Group.

■ You attend the Introduction to Recovery Group.

■ You meet with your program worker to develop and monitor your discharge plan.

■ You participate in preparing and cleaning up after meals.

■ You attend recovery-related appointments (e.g., hunting for housing, treatment interviews).

◇ You and your program worker determine if you are ready for discharge from detox.

■ indicates an action taken by the program worker or the client.
◇ indicates a decision made by the program worker and the client.

Discharge Phase

◇ You and your program worker determine if you are ready for discharge to the community.

■ You are discharged or you move on to post-detox residential support.

■ indicates an action taken by the program worker or the client.
◇ indicates a decision made by the program worker and the client.

Withdrawal Monitoring Checklist (WMC)

Name: _____   Gender: (please circle) M / F   Chart #: _____

This form is completed upon admission if not intoxicated. If the client is intoxicated it is completed 4 hours after admission regardless of the current time; wake the person if he/she is sleeping. It is subsequently completed at breakfast, supper and snack time for the duration of the clients' time in intake. Increase or lack of decrease in severity may be cause for medical referral.

Please circle *one* number for each questionnaire item.   DATE: _____   TIME: _____

AGITATION
No sign of agitation 0
Somewhat more than normal activity 1
Moderately fidgety, shifting position 2
Gross movements /constantly thrashes 3

SWEATING
No sweat visible 0
Just visible sweating, palms moist. 1
Beads of sweat on forehead 2
Drenching sweat on face and chest 3

TREMOR
with arms extended
No tremor 0
Not seen, but can be felt in fingertip 1
Moderate, with arms extended 2
Severe even if arms not extended 3

SLEEP
Sleeps well 0
Broken sleep 1
Difficulty in getting to sleep 2
Insomnia. 3

APPETITE
Good appetite 0
Fair appetite. 1
Poor appetite. 2
No appetite 3

GI DISTURBANCE
No abnormalities. 0
Mild nausea 1
Persistent nausea 2
Vomiting 2 or 3 times. 3

ABDOMINAL CHANGES Ask "Do you have pains in your lower abdomen?"
None reported 0
Waves of cramping pain, some bowel sounds . . 1
Steady bowel pain, or diarrhea, or active bowel . 2

MUSCLE ACHES Ask "Do you have any muscle aches/cramps?"
None reported. 0
Mild muscle pains. 1
Severe muscle pains/contractions 2

ORIENTATION
Knows date and can do serial additions 0
Cannot do serial additions or uncertain of date. . 1
Disoriented for date by 1 or 2 days. 2
Disoriented for date by 3 or more days. 3
Disoriented for place and/or person 4

LEVEL OF CONSCIOUSNESS
Fully alert 0
Slightly drowsy. 1
Very drowsy 2
Roused with difficulty. 3

HALLUCINATIONS
No hallucinations. 0
Auditory hallucinations 1
Visual hallucinations 2
Both auditory and visual hallucinations. 3

MOOD
Cheerful/appropriate. 0
Sometimes low. 1
Often low 2
Despondent. 3

ANXIETY
Finds it easy to relax 0
Finds it difficult to relax. 1
Hardly ever relaxed 2
Cannot relax. 3

COMMENTS

Medical referral needed? (circle) YES / NO → if YES, to where? _____

Medical referral   Date: _____   Time: _____

For what symptoms? _____

Self-discharged?   Date: _____   Time: _____

WMC dec98

HANDOUT 1

INTRODUCTION
TO RECOVERY

Group

GROUP

FACILITATOR'S CHECKLIST AND INFORMATION

Before you start, check that you have the following:
- overheads
    1. Definition of "Group"
    2. Group Roles

Audio/Visual Requirements
- overhead projector and projection screen
- whiteboard and marker

Purpose of the Module

to provide an overview of the nature and purpose of group session, identifying clients' roles and expectations

Objectives

1. to provide background information on the purpose of group for clients in recovery
2. to promote client participation in group
3. to encourage and support clients sharing positive experiences about this and other groups

Special Considerations

- You may want to acknowledge that some clients may have had negative experiences in previous groups. Their experiences, however, may be valuable to this group in that other group members may be able to avoid some of the same pitfalls.
- This module presents information on group dynamics and explains the various roles that participants may assume or be assigned. It is important, however, that these roles do not become "labels" for group members. Rather, the focus should be on self-identification.

NOTE: The facilitator's script and other material to be covered in the group session is in plain text. Instructions for facilitators are presented in **Bold** text.

Getting Started
Each time you start the group, review the following:

Group Norms
- Arrive on time.
- No food or drink is allowed during group sessions.
- Group members will sit in a semi-circle around the whiteboard.
- With the exception of washroom breaks, anyone who wishes to leave the group must first ask the facilitator's permission.
- Any feedback to other members is limited to how you relate to what has been said. Please do not give any advice or make judgmental comments.
- Only one person may speak at a time.
- Any other suggestions for today's group?   **Ask participants.**

How is everyone today?   **Ask around the circle.**

Does anyone have any issues that they wish to raise regarding the Detox Centre?

Introduction

The main purpose of the Introduction to Recovery Group is to exchange information that will help you make informed lifestyle changes and orient you to group in preparation for ongoing treatment.

The purpose of this session, Group, is to discuss the value of group in recovery as well as in day-to-day life.

The Session

Today we'll discuss five components of group:
1. what group is
2. how it can help you
3. how you can contribute to group so that others can learn
    from your experiences
4. how group can work in daily life away from treatment
    and recovery
5. how group works in treatment.

So, let's look at group in three areas: **Show overhead 1 (Definition of "Group")**
• here at this agency
• in other treatment
• in daily life.

This overhead sums up the importance of group. Notice
that this definition also applies to life in general.

This definition really captures the purpose of this module, which
is to discuss the value of group in recovery as
well as in daily life.

Everyone is this group has a unifying relationship with the
other group members, and each of you has or will have other
unifying relationships. So, it appears that all of us will be
in group for the rest of our lives.

First, what is "group" here at our agency?

By the way, this type of group is sometimes referred to as a psychoeducational group. In other words, educational material is presented in a supportive manner by considering the group's particular circumstances, such as the fact that you are here in our agency.

So, besides here, where else will you find group?

Group is one of the most common activities in treatment. If you go for treatment, almost every program will offer group sessions.

Has anyone here attended group in a treatment program?

Can you share what it was like for you? How did it help you?

Well, there are some effective groups in treatment. Our clients often tell us about them. We hope you find one or more groups, and that they are useful to you.

It is not uncommon for recovering people who have long periods of recovery time to discuss their early recovery group experiences, whether they were from a 12-step group or more formal treatment.

Twelve-step programs are one kind of group. Has anyone here learned something useful about recovery from a 12-step group?

So, no one here has received help or remembers help they received from a 12-step program? Well, we hope you'll try these programs because many people have found that they can lead to long-lasting recovery.

In fact, one of our group modules is entitled "The 12 Steps." Perhaps some of you are already familiar with it; others will probably become familiar with it soon.

What are some of the roles that people take on in group?

Perhaps it would be helpful if I first explain what I mean by the term "role." Think of a play. It has a script and the actors take certain roles to make the script come alive.

A similar thing happens here in group. There's no script, but each person often takes a similar role every day. What do you think some of those roles could be?

A therapist named Lawrence Shulman developed these six roles. We use these roles in our work here but other roles are used elsewhere in the helping professions.

Does anyone identify with one or more of these roles?

Has everyone been able to see themselves in these descriptions? If not, can you identify your friends or family members from these definitions?

Wait for and discuss their answers.
If there are no responses, prompt the group by saying:

Can you see why it is useful to identify a person's role in group? Can you explain why to the other group members?

Some answers are:
- **It helps us understand "where a person is coming from."**
- **It helps us identify the need for adjusting the way we talk to each other.**
- **It helps us identify our own purpose or that of others in the group, which, in turn, helps us feel better about being in group.**

Why do you think people often take on these roles?

Steer towards answers that fit the notion that people often take on the role they had when they were children or the role that they assumed when they became adults.

When people assume these roles, what effect does it have on the group? First, let's discuss how these roles can help the group:

Acceptable answers could be:
- **They keep group interesting.**
- **They improve discussion.**
- **They help others to feel included and that what they have to say is appreciated. Some humour is energizing for everyone — <u>staff</u> included.**

How can these roles work against the group?

Answers could be:
- **One person or a few people can dominate the group so that only their agenda is covered.**
- **Discussion gets closed down to what those people want to discuss.**
- **Others feel excluded and closed out of the group.**

Last, let's discuss groups that aren't even about addiction. Where else can you find groups where you have rules like we have here, and where people discuss their problems and try to better understand them?

Answers could be:
- **at work**
- **when taking classes; for example, parenting classes are much like our groups here at 501**
- **decision-making groups at work, in sports and in service clubs.**

Obviously, groups are a valuable tool in helping people in all forms of need. But group is also a major component of life — whether you are seeking help or just interacting with others in day-to-day life.

Wrap Up

What did we discover today about group?

Await clients' responses. Show approval for any good ideas. Add the following points if they are not covered:

We also may have discovered that group is a way:
• to learn to get along with others
• to learn other people's ideas on recovery
• to find out what other people think and say about
  our own ideas
• to learn to respect other people's views, even if
  they sound wrong.

We know that some people have problems with group —
either here, in treatment, in 12-step programs, at work,
or even in sports.

We know that not everyone has an easy time in group —
and sometimes that even includes the group facilitator!
It's hard to listen when:
• you hear things that sound wrong
• someone seems to really misunderstand something
• someone seems to misunderstand who you are,
  what you said, or what you are trying to do.

But group should be a safe place to learn about yourself. It may
seem rocky at the time, but if you look back later and see that
you understood yourself better or someone else better, then
group has helped you.

Definition of "Group"

According to *Webster's Dictionary,*
one definition of group is:

"A number of individuals assembled together
or having some unifying relationship."

Source: *Webster's New Collegiate Dictionary* (1985).

Group Roles

Defensive Member

The member states "It doesn't apply to me" in one or more of the following areas:
1. admitting that a problem exists
2. accepting responsibility for what happens
3. accepting help or suggestions from other group members.

Deviant Member

The member acts differently from all of the others, sometimes in a dramatic and exaggerated way.

The Gatekeeper

Whenever the group starts to discuss a difficult issue, this member does something to prevent the discussion — by changing the subject or creating a disturbance.

Group Roles (cont'd)

The Internal Leader

Although the staff/facilitator may have an agenda, this member strongly asserts what he or she feels is important for the other group members and presents it on their behalf.

The Scapegoat

This member is picked on by the other group members because she or he is unpopular.

Quiet Member

This member may be actively listening but does not participate because he or she is afraid to speak or feels left out.

Source: Shulman, L. (1979). *The Skills of Helping*.

INTRODUCTION TO RECOVERY

Early Recovery

EARLY RECOVERY

FACILITATOR'S CHECKLIST AND INFORMATION

Before you start, check that you have the following:

- overheads
    1. Learning to Manage Your Recovery
    2. HALT
    3. Threats to Recovery
    4. The Day Before My Admission to Detox
- handouts: The Day Before My Admission to Detox

Audio/Visual Requirements

- overhead projector and projection screen
- whiteboard and marker
- handouts of overhead "The Day Before Admission to Detox" and pencils for group members

Purpose of the Module

Many detox clients relapse soon after leaving detox because they are unaware of some of the issues that they will face in early recovery. This module will provide useful information to clients about the first few months of clean time.

Objectives

1. to give background information on what has worked for others in early recovery
2. to encourage clients to prepare themselves for early recovery
3. to encourage and support sharing with others about early recovery
4. to understand the stages of recovery

Special Considerations

- Some clients may believe that their problems are emotional in nature, and consequently may be resistant to the concept of "education." To respond, facilitators may, if appropriate: (a) offer to meet privately to discuss their emotional issues (b) ask them to keep an open mind and see if any ideas presented may help with their recovery (c) explain that thousands of people have recovered successfully because they were helped by an approach that they had originally (and mistakenly) believed was useless, and, (d) if someone suggests that this is the same as a relapse prevention program, explain that relapse prevention is about the details of what you do in a certain situation with certain cues and warnings, while this module is an overview of how early recovery works.

NOTE: The facilitator's script and other material to be covered in the group session is in plain text. Instructions for facilitators are presented in **Bold** text.

Getting Started

Each time you start the group, review the following:

Group Norms
- Arrive on time.
- No food or drink is allowed during group sessions.
- Group members will sit in a semi-circle around the whiteboard.
- With the exception of washroom breaks, anyone who wishes to leave the group must first ask the facilitator's permission.
- Any feedback to other members is limited to how you relate to what has been said. Please do not give any advice or make judgmental comments.
- Only one person may speak at a time.
- Any other suggestions for today's group?   **Ask participants.**

How is everyone today?   **Ask around the circle.**

Does anyone have any issues that they wish to raise regarding the Detox Centre?

Introduction

The main purpose of the Introduction to Recovery Group is to exchange information that will help you make informed lifestyle changes and orient you to the group in preparation for ongoing treatment.

The purpose of this session, Early Recovery, is to discuss some of the issues that you will face in your first few months of recovery.

Our goals for today are:
1. to start discussing our own plans for recovery, because talking is often a good way to start planning
2. to learn some of the pitfalls and problems that can threaten recovery
3. to see some examples of people who have successfully managed their recovery.

The Session

First, let's define "early recovery." Most people who work with those in recovery refer to the first few months as early recovery. This period starts:

1. after detoxification because of the physical, emotional and spiritual changes that can occur then

2. after a firm and serious decision has been made to quit the addiction or addictions

3. when first starting to learn (or relearn after relapse) to fit substance-free practices into daily living.

Some people would argue that recovery begins the moment you decide to change your lifestyle. But for the purpose of our discussion, we will focus on the three points just discussed.

In the next three months or so, what are your plans for recovery?

                                                        Be supportive of clients' plans for recovery.

It's great to hear about your plans. If you want, please comment on them in relation to what we are discussing here today.

Throughout your recovery you will be asked to share your experiences and plans for recovery and you will also hear other people's plans. If someone has recovery plans that you don't think will work, or that you even think are wrong, what's the right thing for you to do?

1. What won't work for you might be the best thing for someone else.

2. Your recovery plan might be a disaster for someone else.

Try to think of a time when you were trying to stay clean, but you started using again. Can you explain how you knew that your recovery was at risk?

This graph shows how some people manage to stay in recovery. It demonstrates the need to identify vulnerable times and how to swing back up into the supportive times.

Notice how life has its ups and downs! This applies not only to substance abuse, but also to all areas of our lives. Everyone experiences these ups and downs. Our goal is to identify when they occur and to determine the causes of the down times.

What could be some of the causes for this downward turn?

Without going into a large-scale relapse-prevention session, we want you to see an example of a simple idea that many people in recovery use effectively.

Has anybody seen this HALT warning before today? Can anybody identify the words that each letter stands for?

Point to where someone is going down towards relapse:

The concept is that if we let ourselves experience two or more of these negative feelings at any one time, we are on our way down the graph. What are some other threats or threatening combinations that we need to be aware of?

What are some examples of grief issues? Some recovering people state that they feel like they lost their best friend when they stopped using drugs or alcohol.

Another issue of concern is depression. If depression is identified as a serious ongoing concern, you need to seek medical help.

What are some of the symptoms of depression?

Traumatic events can involve a variety of things. What is traumatic for one person may not be traumatic for another. It is up to you to identify events that can cause you pain.

Another important issue that is not on the overhead involves the use of time. Can anyone discuss the use of time in recovery?

Take a few minutes and fill in the chart. We won't discuss it right now but we will use it later in the session.

So, again, the goal is for us to intervene in our downward turn as soon as possible ...at a 4 as opposed to waiting for "Uh! Oh!" and subsequent relapse.

Many people learn to recognize earlier and earlier that they are on the way down, and they do something about it.

What are some ways to intervene on our own behalf?

Do you feel as though you have learned one or two new ways of coping?

Now, let's go back to our handouts. In the blank area, write down your activities while you are here in this program.

There should be a significant change for most of you. What does this change mean? It means you can change and you have shown that you can direct the flow of your own ups and downs.

Thanks for participating in today's session.

Learning to Manage Your Recovery

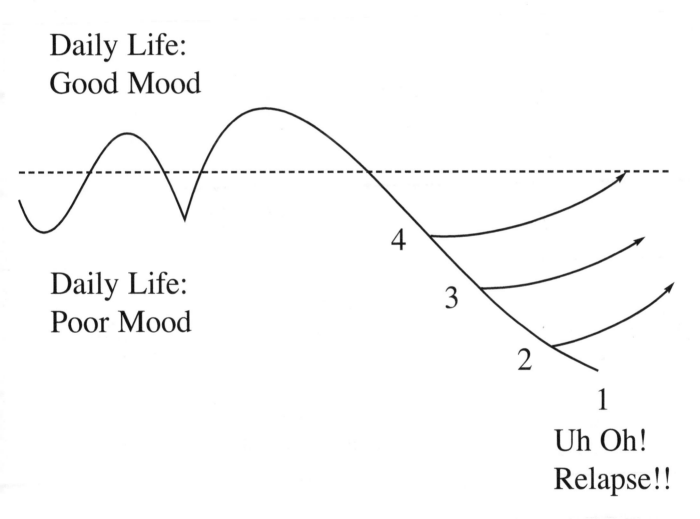

Daily Life:
Good Mood

Daily Life:
Poor Mood

4

3

2

1

Uh Oh!
Relapse!!

H **A** **L** **T**
u n o i
n g n r
g r e e
r y l d
y   y

—————

From 12 Step Slogans

Threats to Recovery

- grief

- depression

- traumatic events

Q **How do these threats put recovery at risk?**

A **In two ways:**

1. Your old patterns are to use or drink to deal with them.

2. Re-learning **not** to drink or use may be difficult because perhaps society, perhaps your family, or perhaps your friends may encourage you to do so.

What will you do?

The Day Before
My Admission to Detox

	Activities
Midnight	
1 a.m.	
2 a.m.	
3 a.m.	
4 a.m.	
5 a.m.	
6 a.m.	
7 a.m.	
8 a.m.	
9 a.m.	
10 a.m.	
11 a.m.	
Noon	
1 p.m.	
2 p.m.	
3 p.m.	
4 p.m.	
5 p.m.	
6 p.m.	
7 p.m.	
8 p.m.	
9 p.m.	
10 p.m.	
11 p.m.	

The Day Before
My Admission to Detox

	Activities
Midnight	
1 a.m.	
2 a.m.	
3 a.m.	
4 a.m.	
5 a.m.	
6 a.m.	
7 a.m.	
8 a.m.	
9 a.m.	
10 a.m.	
11 a.m.	
Noon	
1 p.m.	
2 p.m.	
3 p.m.	
4 p.m.	
5 p.m.	
6 p.m.	
7 p.m.	
8 p.m.	
9 p.m.	
10 p.m.	
11 p.m.	

INTRODUCTION
TO RECOVERY

The 12 Steps

THE 12 STEPS

FACILITATOR'S CHECKLIST AND INFORMATION

Before you start, check that you have the following:	• overheads
	    1. 12-Step Groups
	    2. Facts about the 12 Steps
	    3. Anonymity
	    4. The 12 Steps of Alcoholics Anonymous

Audio/Visual Requirements	• overhead projector and projection screen • whiteboard and marker
Purpose of the Module	Many clients may already have or need experience with the 12 steps; therefore this module will clarify the 12 steps as a possible tool in recovery.
Objectives	1. to provide background information on the 12 steps 2. to promote the 12 steps as a viable option for clients 3. to encourage and support sharing at a 12-step level
Special Considerations	• Some clients may have had negative experiences with 12-step groups. • In order to be an informed resource for this module, ideally the facilitator should have attended at least one 12-step meeting in the past year. • This topic will likely prompt clients to share their experiences. If a client's sharing appears to be positively affecting the group, do not discourage it. Don't worry if you don't manage to cover all the material — it only means that the spirit of the 12 steps took hold for this particular session.

NOTE: The facilitator's script and other material to be covered in the group session is in plain text. Instructions for facilitators are presented in **Bold** text.

Getting Started
Each time you start the group, review the following:

Group Norms
• Arrive on time.
• No food or drink is allowed during group sessions.
• Group members will sit in a semi-circle around the whiteboard.
• With the exception of washroom breaks, anyone who wishes to leave the group must first ask the facilitator's permission.
• Any feedback to other members is limited to how you relate to what has been said. Please do not give any advice or make judgmental comments.
• Only one person may speak at a time.
• Any other suggestions for today's group?   **Ask participants.**

How is everyone today?   **Ask around the circle.**

Does anyone have any issues that they wish to raise regarding the Detox Centre?

Introduction

The main purpose of the Introduction to Recovery Group is to exchange information that will help you make informed lifestyle changes and orient you to group in preparation for ongoing treatment.

The purpose of this session, 12 Steps, is to discuss the value of this approach as one component of treatment.

The Session

Has anyone here ever attended a 12-step meeting of any kind? If so, can you summarize your experience (good or bad) in a couple of sentences? If your experience was negative, please do not try to cloud the judgment of others.

Discuss three or four responses. Explain that others will have an opportunity to contribute later in the discussion. Explain why this facility/program believes that the 12 steps are important.

Treatment centres use different approaches and tools to promote recovery — ranging from spiritual-based programs to programs focused more on a psychological approach to wellness. Because you are here for only a short time, we need to be conscious of presenting information on the most relevant approaches. Therefore, we offer a group module on the 12 steps because this approach is immediately available to you, in this and most other communities, and you can choose to use the information right away.

Show overhead 1 (12-Step Groups).

Why are 12-step groups so accessible?

Where are 12-step meetings offered in this community? (locations and types — Alcoholics Anonymous, Narcotics Anonymous, etc.)

Does anyone know who was the other co-founder of AA? (Dr. Bob S.) Can you imagine what it must have been like for two guys to start AA back in the 1930s? So, the 12 steps have been around for a long time. How many other 12-step groups are there besides the obvious ones, such as AA, NA and CA?

Let's discuss why these programs are usually referred to as "Anonymous," and the significance of anonymity in general.

Can anyone share his or her thoughts on the above statement and perhaps reflect how it applies to us in this program?

Take note of the use of the term "we" in step one; in practice, the "we" can be placed at the beginning of every step. The steps also refer to "us," "ourselves," and so on.

The "we" is emphasized because it is symbolic of one human being reaching out to another. If anyone here has prior experience in recovery, you have probably concluded that the task of recovery is something we cannot do alone. If it were possible to do it alone, none of you would likely be here.

The steps are numbered because they are meant to be completed in order. In other words, you should be completely committed to step 1 before moving on to step 2. At this point it is important to remind you that that what we are discussing today will not take the place of or preclude anything you have already experienced regarding the 12 steps. This is not a 12-step group. If you want to find out more about the 12 steps, get involved by attending the meetings.

Wrap Up

What did we discover today about the steps?

Await clients' responses. Show approval for any good ideas. Add the following points if they are not covered:

We may have also discovered that the steps are:
• accessible (almost every community offers 12-step groups)
• worthwhile (many people have been helped by such programs)
• used when entering recovery, throughout recovery, in follow-up and during continuing care after more formal treatment
• a good way to get connected in a community; 12-step groups help us feel as though we're not alone.

However, we must also recognize that the 12 steps are not necessarily for everyone. Each person is unique and has different needs. But one of the main benefits of the 12 steps is that they will always be there if you want to explore them.

12-Step Groups

The Largest and Most Accessible Continuing Care Support Group

Facts about the 12 Steps

- They were written in 1938 by Bill W., co-founder of AA.

- The program evolved out of a need for unity and simplicity.

- Today many self-help groups have adopted the 12 Steps.

Anonymity

Anonymity is the spiritual foundation of all our traditions, ever reminding us to place principles before personalities.

Source: W., Bill. (1996). *Twelve Steps and Twelve Traditions.*

The 12 Steps of Alcoholics Anonymous

1 We admitted we were powerless over alcohol – that our lives had become unmanageable.

2 Came to believe that a power greater than ourselves could restore us to sanity.

3 Made a decision to turn our will and our lives over to the care of God *as we understood him*.

4 Made a searching and fearless moral inventory of ourselves.

5 Admitted to God, to ourselves and to another human being the exact nature of our wrongs.

6 Were entirely ready to have God remove all these defects of character.

7 Humbly asked him to remove our shortcomings.

8 Made a list of all persons we had harmed and became willing to make amends to them all.

9 Made direct amends to such people wherever possible, except when to do so would injure them or others.

10 Continued to take personal inventory and when we were wrong, promptly admitted it.

11 Sought through prayer and meditation to improve our conscious contact with God *as we understood him,* praying only for knowledge of his will for us and the power to carry that out.

12 Having had a spiritual awakening as the result of these steps we tried to carry this message to others and to practice these principles in all our affairs.

OVERHEAD 4

INTRODUCTION
TO RECOVERY

General Wellness

GENERAL WELLNESS

FACILITATOR'S CHECKLIST AND INFORMATION

Before you start, check that you have the following:	• overheads

1. The Stages of Sleep   4. Food for Healing
2. Managing Stress   5. The Immune System
3. Food for Energy   6. Threats to the Immune System

Audio/Visual Requirements

• overhead projector and projection screen
• whiteboard and marker

Purpose of the Module

to provide an overview of how clients can increase their own wellness

Objectives

1. to encourage clients to seek the enjoyable feelings that are a part of wellness
2. to teach principles of wellness, especially around areas likely to affect people with addictions
3. to provide interesting new information on wellness — information that clients probably won't find elsewhere during early recovery

Special Considerations

• Some clients may challenge or reject the material presented in this module. There can be several reasons for their resistance:

    a) The client believes that he or she is well educated on these issues through previous attempts at recovery and treatment.

Facilitator's response: **"We had to prepare this module for everybody, not just people who have already been exposed to the information. Please be patient with the group and the process."**

    b) The client prefers to attribute most ill health to external factors such as heredity and the environment.

Facilitator's response: **"Regardless of your heredity or the environment you are in, there are things you can do to make yourself healthier, rather than simply doing nothing."**

    c) The client feels threatened by anything that suggests that he or she should change his or her habits.

Facilitator's response: **"You may not feel that this material is relevant to you, but it might help others, so please let them listen and decide for themselves."**

NOTE: The facilitator's script and other material to be covered in the group session is in plain text. Instructions for facilitators are presented in **Bold** text.

Getting Started
Each time you start the group, review the following:

Group Norms
- Arrive on time.
- No food or drink is allowed during group sessions.
- Group members will sit in a semi-circle around the whiteboard.
- With the exception of washroom breaks, anyone who wishes to leave the group must first ask the facilitator's permission.
- Any feedback to other members is limited to how you relate to what has been said. Please do not give any advice or make judgmental comments.
- Only one person may speak at a time.
- Any other suggestions for today's group?   **Ask participants.**

How is everyone today?   **Ask around the circle.**

Does anyone have any issues that they wish to raise regarding the Detox Centre?

Introduction

The main purpose of the Introduction to Recovery Group is to exchange information that will help you make informed lifestyle changes and orient you to group in preparation for ongoing treatment.

The purpose of this session, Wellness, is to help you identify periods in your life when you have felt good — physically, emotionally or both — and to provide practical information on ways to help yourself feel well.

The Session

Does anyone have any ideas about what we mean by the term "wellness"?

Discuss responses.

What are some things that make us feel well?

Today we will be discussing sleep, stress, nutrition, the immune system, and risk factors.

Sleep

First, let's talk about sleep. How are your sleeping habits?

Let's try to remember a time when sleep was really great — when it felt really good. How did it feel? When was that? What do you think made your sleep then so great?

Let's look at what happens in healthy sleep.

This is what happens when you have sleep that feels good and that rests your body and your mind.

Does anyone here believe alcohol helps you sleep?

A little alcohol will help you fall asleep easier, but the rest of your sleep will be shallow and not restful. You will still be tired when you wake up. A lot of alcohol will make all of your sleep shallow and broken. This loss of sound sleep can contribute to delirium. Also, your immune system will become weaker and less able to fight off disease.

Stress

Drinking heavily and taking drugs are among the most stressful ways that anyone can live. What does your body do when it's under stress? How does it respond to stress?

Record answers on the whiteboard. Add any of the following that may have been overlooked.
- **heart rate increases**
- **blood pressure increases**
- **rate of breathing increases**
- **muscles become tense, ready for action**
- **body releases glucose for quick energy**
- **body releases adrenaline for energy and endurance**

Any one of these processes is exhausting for your body. Their long-term effects wear you down. You get tired more easily, you get sick easier, you get angry or depressed easier. Stress can kill you.

If you work hard on your recovery, but the stress on you increases — on the job, at home, from relatives, from wanting to drink or use drugs again — does that mean that you will relapse?

Show overhead 2 (Managing Stress).
To avoid distraction, show only one section of the overhead at a time.

Nutrition

There's a separate session on nutrition so today we'll just touch very briefly on two topics: food for energy and food for healing.

Modern society encourages us to take things to give us energy — things like certain drugs and types of food that supposedly create energy. But, in reality, many of the things we take actually sap our energy. Can you name some things that supposedly give us energy?

Wait for answers and record them on the whiteboard. Then supply whichever items were overlooked.
- **caffeine**   • **tobacco**
- **sugar**   • **fatty snacks**
- **alcohol or drugs**

The short lift of energy that we get from these things — for a matter of minutes or hours — is pulled down by a longer period of lower energy.

The next overhead shows some nutritional strategies that will give you energy. Can you suggest some energy-building strategies?

Wait for responses and then show overhead 3 (Food for Energy).

Now let's look at "Food for Healing." If you wanted to eat foods to help your body heal faster — and long-term recovery involves some bodily healing — what types of things would you drink and eat?

Wait for some responses and then show overhead 4 (Food for Healing).

Note: It may be difficult to implement some of these changes under your present circumstances but this knowledge will help you in the near future.

The Immune System

The overhead on the stages of sleep showed us that during deep sleep our immune system works harder and helps us stay healthy. Does anyone know what the immune system is?

Basically, your immune system helps your body fight off infections and other diseases. If you didn't have an immune system — or if it gets completely run down and weak — you could die from just a cold.

But many people fight off or live with many diseases that are much more severe than a cold — cancer, tuberculosis, Hepatitis A, B and C, and HIV/AIDS, for example. How? Here are just a few details on how your immune system works.

The immune system has two jobs: it identifies cells as either "self" or "non-self" and as either "safe" or "dangerous." For example: some grass pollens in the air are breathed in, and are identified as "non-self" but are not "fought." But, other grass pollens may be identified as "non-self" and are fought with strong allergic reactions, or "hay fever."

The immune system does this because the white blood cells and protein molecules cruise the bloodstream and lymph system (the lymph nodes in your neck, armpits and groin swell when infected) looking for dangerous "non-self" cells to attack and kill.

So, your own immune system is just waiting and ready to help protect your body. It's like an Emergency Response Team against any disease.

All your immune system asks, each day, is for some good rest, some good food and drink, and some positive, relaxing thoughts.

Show overhead 6 (Threats to the Immune System).

Risk Factors

Different diseases tend to concentrate in different groups of people. For example, do many elderly people get chicken pox?

No, children tend to catch chicken pox.

Now, for someone who has a serious drinking or drug problem, can you name some diseases that that person might be more likely to come down with?

Keeping with our approach of finding ways to make sure we feel better, let's now look at one the diseases that you just mentioned.

OK, if you had the choice of contracting _____ ,

would you go somewhere and say "Give me a dose of _____ ?"

You've just given us good reasons why you do, in fact, have some say in, and some control over, your life. It's just too easy to say "My life is out of control" and to mistakenly believe that you aren't in control. And maintaining your own wellness, protecting your own wellness, doesn't cost you anything — not a nickel. And you can do it anywhere, anywhere you live.

There's another way to look at our theme today. It's called harm reduction and it involves looking at how you can reduce the harms that occur to you.

Looking after yourself in any way — sleeping better, eating better, handling stress — it's all harm reduction.

Wrap Up

Now, to summarize the session, we discussed paying attention to what makes you feel well and how to have better sleep, energy and thoughts, and trying to feel better by reducing the harms to yourself — which is called harm reduction.

Before we close, do you have any questions?

Thank you for participating today. We hope that you will start feeling better by deciding to live a way that *feels* better and better — whether you do it with big changes or just small gradual improvements.

The Stages of Sleep

Type of Sleep	Characteristics
Stage 1: Light Sleep	ABOUT 10 MINUTES drift in and out of hazy, foggy sleep
Stage 2: Intermediate Sleep	ABOUT 20 MINUTES much harder to wake up
Stage 3: Deep Sleep or Slow Wave Sleep (SWS) ■ This is deep, restful and restoring sleep. ■ "I slept well" happens here.	A FEW MINUTES TO ONE HOUR large slow brainwaves ■ Your immune system works harder now than during the rest of your sleep. ■ *Any* caffeine or nicotine 12 hours before weakens or even eliminates this stage of sleep.
(back to) **Stage 2**	BRIEF, MINUTES ONLY
Stage 3	AS ABOVE
Rapid Eye Movement (REM) Sleep	Most dreaming occurs here, face and fingers twitch.
Then, repeating cycles of: Stage 2 and Stage 3 and REM Sleep	FOUR TO SIX CYCLES THROUGH THE NIGHT

Sources: Dotto, L. (1990). *Asleep In the Fast Lane: The Impact of Sleep on Work;* Coren, S. (1996). *Sleep Thieves.*

Managing Stress

There are three ways to manage stress:

1 Remove the stressor.

Examples:

On the job: Change jobs, change bosses, change co-workers.

At home: Leave home, separate or divorce.

Relatives: Move away, break off relations.

Addictions: Can you move to where there are no drugs or alcohol?

2 Change the stressor.

Examples:

On the job: Talk with the difficult co-worker or boss and negotiate new ways to work together.

At home: Seek counselling and learn new ways to communicate and relate to each other.

Relatives: Discuss how to understand each other better.

Addictions: ?

3 Change your response to the stressor.

Examples:

On the job: Learn skills in negotiation, assertiveness, relaxation – through classes, books or TV courses.

At home and with relatives: Work hard at understanding and communicating well, perhaps seek counselling here too.

Addictions: Gain self-knowledge through 12-step or other groups; learn relaxation, assertiveness or negotiation techniques from classes, books or TV; perhaps seek counselling.

Adapted from: British Columbia Ministry of Health. (1992). *Choosing Wellness.*

Food for Energy

1 A good breakfast gets your metabolism going for the whole day.

2 Choose whole-grain bread, buns and pitas instead of ones made with white flour. Whole grains have the fibre, iron and B vitamins to sustain your energy.

3 Cut back on coffee, tea and other caffeinated drinks. Three cups a day or more can leave you dehydrated, jittery and low on iron in your blood.

4 Taking more vitamins or minerals than your body needs won't give you more energy. Check with your doctor, pharmacist, or a registered nutritionist or dietician first.

5 Cut back on processed and fast foods. High levels of sugar, salt and fats will slow you down.

6 All fruits have a special kind of sugar called fructose that keeps your blood sugar level higher longer than manufactured sugar, or sucrose.

Adapted from: British Columbia Ministry of Health. (1992). *Choosing Wellness*.

Food for Healing

1 Drink lots of fluids – six to eight cups per day – of juice, milk or water. Decrease the amount of sugar added to drinks as much as possible.

2 Eat more dark-green or yellow/orange vegetables and fruit.

3 Switch to eating whole grains as much as possible. Add wheat germ to cereals and to home-made bread or muffins.

4 Eat lots of home-made soup made with fresh vegetables and legumes (dry beans, dry peas, lentils).

Adapted from: British Columbia Ministry of Health. (1992). *Choosing Wellness*.

The Immune System

The immune system has two main jobs:

1 It identifies cells as either "self" or "non-self" and "safe" or "dangerous."

2 It fights off dangerous "non-self" cells.

Source: Rees, A. & Wiley, C. (Eds.). (1993). *Personal Health Reporter.*

Threats to the Immune System

The immune system is weakened by the following factors:

- poor sleep

- poor diet or dehydration

- prolonged stress

- lack of exercise

- long illness

- smoking

- pollutants in the air, water and food.

Nutrition

NUTRITION

FACILITATOR'S CHECKLIST AND INFORMATION

Before you start, check that you have the following:

- 13 "True/False" overheads
- a sheet to cover answer portion of overheads. To present the overheads effectively, see the following points:
    1. Before placing the transparency on the projector, place the blank sheet behind the overhead covering the bottom part below the dotted line.
    2. Read the question aloud.
    3. Encourage discussion of clients' responses.
    4. To answer the question, pull down the sheet enough to reveal the "True/False" — but not the whole answer.
    5. Next, read the answer, using your own words. If you simply showed the answer, group members would be distracted and won't focus on you.
    6. Encourage discussion about the "correct" answer or answers.
- copies of the Canada Food Guides for all group members
- copies of the Nutritional Check List for all group members

Audio/Visual Requirements

- overhead projector and projection screen
- whiteboard and marker

Purpose of the Module

to present basic information about the importance of healthy eating

Objectives

1. to initiate an informal and supportive discussion of clients' food/nutritional preferences, providing reassurance that they won't be scolded, corrected or made to feel ashamed
2. to present some of the adverse effects of addiction on their nutrition-related health (Other addiction-related diseases will be covered in another module.)
3. to present ways in which clients can improve their food choices

Special Considerations

- Some clients may have specific dietary needs or health issues, such as diabetes, which are related to nutrition. If this is the case, adapt the presentation accordingly.
- Some clients may have special psychological or emotional issues related to eating or the social context of eating. If this is the case, adapt the presentation to address their concerns.

NOTE: The facilitator's script and other material to be covered in the group session is in plain text. Instructions for facilitators are presented in **Bold** text.

Getting Started

Each time you start the group, review the following:

Group Norms
- Arrive on time.
- No food or drink is allowed during group sessions.
- Group members will sit in a semi-circle around the whiteboard.
- With the exception of washroom breaks, anyone who wishes to leave the group must first ask the facilitator's permission.
- Any feedback to other members is limited to how you relate to what has been said. Please do not give any advice or make judgmental comments.
- Only one person may speak at a time.
- Any other suggestions for today's group?   **Ask participants.**

How is everyone today?   **Ask around the circle.**

Does anyone have any issues that they wish to raise regarding the Detox Centre?

Introduction

The main purpose of the Introduction to Recovery Group is to exchange information that will help you make informed lifestyle changes and orient you to group in preparation for ongoing treatment.

The purpose of this session, Nutrition, is to discuss the importance of nutrition in recovery and to identify ways that you may be able to introduce good nutrition into recovery plans.

We will discuss four key areas today:
1. your eating habits and your attitudes about eating
2. nutrition in relation to substance use/abuse
3. designing your own plan for healthful eating
4. social aspects of eating and nutrition.

The Session

Let's start with the first area: your eating habits. In the few days before you came to this centre, what were your eating habits like?

Do you think you have ever had really good eating habits?

What were some of the smart eating choices you made, even if they were only for a short time?

Do you think food helps recovery? In what ways?

What kinds of foods would you like to eat while you are in recovery?

Now let's look at our second point — food in relation to substance use/abuse.

During our discussion we will be looking at a series of overheads. These overheads are a series of true/false questions.

Using the approach outlined above, work through overheads 1 to 13. For overhead 1, you may want to explain what a diuretic is.

Now, let's discuss our third point and discuss how you would design a good eating lifestyle once you are back in your own place.

Distribute copies of the *Canada Food Guide*. Explain that the portions listed depend on the age and size of the person — the lowest are for children and the highest are for teenagers.

What would be the easiest food group for you to do well in? What would be the next easiest? What would be the hardest? What might help you to eat better in that group?

Let's turn now to our fourth point — the social aspects of eating.

Eating is a highly social activity. In most cultures around the world, mealtime is when a group of people who know each other, or otherwise want to get to know each other, come together.

Does anyone have any comments about eating with other people or eating alone?

Are any of these social aspects related to your recovery?

Does anyone else see your recovery as related to whom you eat with?

Recovery Diets

Some people have made changes to their eating habits that they believe made an important difference in maintaining their recovery. However, we can't recommend these changes because they haven't been approved by the medical profession and we haven't had personal experience with them.

But if you would like more information, inquire at your 12-step group (or at several if you attend more than one 12-step group) and then consult your doctor.

Thank you for participating in today's session. We hope the information presented will help you make positive changes to your choices about nutrition.

Detoxification will occur as fast as your body can metabolize (process) toxins (poisons) and there is nothing much you can do other than rest and sleep.

TRUE ❏   FALSE ❏

FALSE

You can help your body to clean itself out and heal itself by eating well and drinking at least six glasses of water per day.

Coffee, tea, soft drinks and other diuretics don't count towards the total of six glasses. Only water and non-sugared drinks count.

Source: Kart, Marjorie and Sherry Smith. *Stop Smoking Program: Facilitators' Guide* (1993) Toronto: Addiction Research Foundation, page 4.1.

OVERHEAD 1

When you drink a can of pop, you take in about nine teaspoons of sugar.

TRUE ❏   FALSE ❏

TRUE

Source: Kart, M. and Sherry S. (1993). *Stop Smoking Program for Women: Facilitators' Guide*.

Substance withdrawal and recovery are so demanding — physically, mentally and spiritually — that to withdraw from sugar, caffeine and tobacco at the same time is more than we can handle. So, work on your recovery — one drug at a time

TRUE ❏   FALSE ❏

There are three good answers here.

1. "One drug at a time" is conventional wisdom for many people who suffer tremendously in withdrawal and can't even imagine taking on more punishment.

2. "Withdraw from your main drug(s) and from sugar and caffeine" is the advice of Dr. Joan Larson, who has a successful practice with people who have addictions. She finds that sugar (for alcoholics) and caffeine addictions act as triggers and as prime threats to recovery from drugs.

   Once her clients are withdrawn from sugar and caffeine, they can then more easily drop the nicotine habit.

   But she also suggests becoming aware of your nicotine intake by counting how many cigarettes you smoke each day.

3. Withdrawing from your main drug(s) and from tobacco at the same time has worked well in some treatment programs, even with people who at first couldn't imagine taking on both of these challenges at once.

Source: Larson, J. (1992). *Alcoholism — The Biochemical Connection.*

OVERHEAD 3

Nutrition-related health problems happen more with alcoholics than with other serious substance abusers.

TRUE ❑   FALSE ❑

FALSE

A common stereotype is that alcoholics suffer from serious liver defects while people who abuse other drugs will experience only minor nutritional problems.

In fact, *all* addictions that cause people to prefer their substance to healthful food and regular eating habits cause many similar health problems, all of which are related to malnutrition. These include:
• nausea • diarrhea • loss of appetite • dental decay
• anxiety • depression • fatigue • frequent minor illnesses • insomnia.

Source: Beasley, J. & Knightly, S. (1993). *Food for Recovery.*

Low blood sugar (hypoglycemia) is an important factor in relapse for recovering alcoholics.

TRUE ❑   FALSE ❑

Perhaps TRUE, although there is some debate here.

The "yes" side states that a large percentage of alcoholics suffer from hypoglycemia and that this creates danger for their recovery because it results in low energy, irritability, depression, difficulty concentrating, and sugar cravings that lead to alcohol cravings. Dr. Bob S. (co-founder of AA) was a physician and he supported this view.

The "no" side states that many people who seem to be hypoglycemic are not really suffering from that disease. So we don't know if they are really and truly hypoglycemic because the tests aren't done properly.

Sources: Ketcham, K. & Mueller, L. (1983). *Eating Right to Live Sober;* Beasley, J. & Knightly, S. (1993). *Food for Recovery;* Finnegan, J. & Gray, D. (1990). *Recovery from Addiction;* Larson, J. (1992). *Alcoholism — The Biochemical Connection.*

Most people gain weight when they quit smoking.

TRUE ❏   FALSE ❏

TRUE

Usually there is a minimal weight gain.

If you quit smoking and gain weight, you are just trading one health problem for another.

TRUE ❏   FALSE ❏

FALSE

The health hazard of smoking is much, much greater than for gaining weight.

To equal the health risk of a pack-a-day smoking habit, you would have to gain
55 kilograms.

Source: Kart, M. & Sherry S. (1993). *Stop Smoking Program for Women: Facilitators' Guide*.

Over 50 per cent of the calories in chocolate come from fat.

TRUE ❏   FALSE ❏

TRUE

Source: Kart, M. & Sherry S. (1993). *Stop Smoking Program for Women: Facilitators' Guide*.

During recovery, the body needs more protein-rich foods for energy.

TRUE ❏   FALSE ❏

FALSE

Protein's role is to build and repair muscle tissues, not to provide energy. The best way to replace the muscle lost due to substance abuse is by eating a high-carbohydrate diet (to conserve protein), exercising and allowing time for your muscle mass to recover. Most people eat enough protein to satisfy their needs. If you eat more protein than you need, the excess is converted to fat. To determine appropriate protein and carbohydrate levels, see your registered dietician.

Source: Daniel, E. (1991). Nutritional implications in recovery from substance abuse.

If you need to lower your blood cholesterol, you should avoid cholesterol-rich foods.

TRUE ❏   FALSE ❏

FALSE

The key to lowering blood cholesterol is to eat less fat, especially saturated fat, and to increase your intake of complex carbohydrates such as grain products. Fibre-rich foods such as whole-grain products, legumes, vegetables and fruit are also emphasized.

Source: Canadian Dietetic Association. (1993). *Nutrition Checkup for Women*.

White spots or ridges on your fingernails indicate a vitamin or mineral deficiency.

TRUE ❑   FALSE ❑

FALSE

These little white spots are usually the result of a minor injury — such as a minor blow to the finger-nail. Longitudinal ridges are not uncommon and may be hereditary.

Source: Milk Marketing Board. (1990). Fact Sheets.

During recovery, taking a vitamin and mineral supplement will provide extra energy.

TRUE ❏   FALSE ❏

FALSE, but also somewhat TRUE

Vitamins cannot give you pep and energy because they have no calories. Vitamins and minerals are responsible for many important functions in the body, and work in harmony with macro-nutrients (protein, carbohydrates, and fat) to assist in metabolism.

During recovery a well-balanced diet may not supply all the vitamins and minerals that you need for healing. A vitamin B complex with zinc and magnesium may benefit those in early recovery.

Source: Daniel, E. (1991). Nutritional implications in recovery from substance abuse; Marsano, L. (1993). Alcohol and malnutrition.

What you eat can affect your mood.

TRUE ☐   FALSE ☐

TRUE

Food is important to basic brain activity. The composition of each meal and snack can make a difference to how much you eat, how you feel and how soon you want to eat again. Choosing the proper proportion of carbohydrate, protein and fat in the meal or snack has significance beyond calorie counting.

For example, after you eat a carbohydrate meal or snack (e.g., fruit, vegetables, breads, pastas, rice or potatoes) there is an increase in a brain chemical that induces sleepiness and relaxation (serotonin).

When you eat protein, the brain picture changes and there is an increased production of another brain chemical that influences alertness and concentration (dopamine). Learning to balance your food intake will have a profound impact on your recovery.

Source: Fernstrom, J. (1994). Dietary amino acids and brain function; Biery, Janet et al. (1991). Alcohol craving in rehabilitation: assessment of nutrition therapy.

Nutritional Check List   Date: _____

Use this checklist to find out if you or someone you know is at nutritional risk.

Read the statements below. Circle the number in the "yes" column for those that apply to you or someone you know. For each "yes" answer, score that number. Total your nutritional score.

	Yes
I have an illness or condition that made me change the kind and/or amount of food I eat.	2
I eat fewer than two meals per day.	3
I eat few fruits or vegetables, or milk products.	2
I have three or more drinks or beer, liquor or wine almost every day.	2
I have tooth or mouth problems that make it hard for me to eat.	2
I don't always have enough money to buy the food I need.	4
I eat alone most of the time.	1
I take three or more different prescribed or over-the-counter drugs a day.	1
Without wanting to, I have lost or gained 10 pounds in the last six months.	2
I am not always able to shop, cook, and/or feed myself.	2
	Total

Total your nutritional score. If it is:

0–2   *Good!* Recheck your nutritional score in six months.

3–5   *You are at moderate nutritional risk.* See what can be done to improve your eating habits and lifestyle. Recheck your nutritional score in three months.

6 or more   *You are at high nutritional risk.* Make an appointment to see a physician.

Adapted from materials developed and distributed by the Nutritional Screening Initiative, a project of:
American Academy of Family Physicians, the American Dietetic Association, and National Council on the Aging, Inc.

HANDOUT 1

●●●

Canada's Food Guide

[insert printed copy from supply]

●●●

INTRODUCTION TO RECOVERY

Relaxation for Recovery

RELAXATION

FOR RECOVERY

FACILITATOR'S CHECKLIST AND INFORMATION

Before you start, check that you have the following:

- optional video entitled "Sick of Stress"
    (ARF #1102 available through Audio-Vision,
        3 Morningside Place, Norwalk, CT, USA, 06854)
- optional audiotape entitled "Progressive Muscular Relaxation"
    (ARF #5000; any similar audiotape will be useful; the purpose
        is to give an example of how relaxation audiotapes sound)
- if available, pillows and floor pads for the relaxation exercises

Audio/Visual Requirements

- monitor and VCR
- cassette player

Purpose of the Module

- to offer insights about the role of relaxation in recovery by
    discussing how relaxation can help clients deal with stresses
    that lead to relapse
- to provide information on how to carry out specific relaxation
    techniques by watching the video
- to reinforce the theory by practising relaxation techniques
    during today's group

Objectives

1. to provide background information on stress and relaxation
    techniques
2. to encourage clients to think of how relaxation exercises
    can help their recovery
3. to encourage and support sharing with others around
    this topic
4. to demonstrate the effectiveness of using audiotapes
    as a relaxation aid

NOTE: The facilitator's script and other material to be covered in the group session is in plain text.
Instructions for facilitators are presented in **Bold** text.

Getting Started
Each time you start the group, review the following:

Group Norms
- Arrive on time.
- No food or drink is allowed during group sessions.
- Group members will sit in a semi-circle around the whiteboard.
- With the exception of washroom breaks, anyone who wishes to leave the group must first ask the facilitator's permission.
- Any feedback to other members is limited to how you relate to what has been said. Please do not give any advice or make judgmental comments.
- Only one person may speak at a time.
- Any other suggestions for today's group?   **Ask participants.**

How is everyone today?   **Ask around the circle.**

Does anyone have any issues that they wish to raise regarding the Detox Centre?

Introduction

The main purpose of the Introduction to Recovery Group is to exchange information that will help you make informed lifestyle changes and orient you to group in preparation for ongoing treatment.

The purpose of this session, "Relaxation for Recovery," is to teach you how to use relaxation techniques to deal with stress.

Although you'll hear about some detailed relaxation techniques that are taught by professionals, we encourage you to take the information presented and use it as you need it, perhaps changing it to suit your unique needs.

The Session

Our goals for today are:
1. to better understand how stress negatively affects your health.
2. to learn specific relaxation techniques
3. to try some of these techniques — but only if you choose to
4. to learn to take the facts presented and adapt them to suit
   your needs

Has anyone here ever learned any relaxation techniques?

Show approval for responses and add comments as appropriate.

People in recovery need to develop alternative responses to stress other than drinking or taking other drugs. Relaxation strategies are vital to a comprehensive program of recovery.

Did these techniques help you to relax?

Aside from your personal experiences, what have you heard about relaxation techniques?

Aside from the people who spoke earlier, has anyone else actually used these relaxation techniques?

Appropriate Expectations

People who teach relaxation techniques don't claim that it is easy and will happen in just one sitting. Anyone who has tried relaxation techniques knows that you have to practise them several times a week, and, over a period of several weeks, you slowly get better at it.

So if you want to have techniques available to you to deal with stress when you experience it, you need to start now to build up your ability.

If someone thinks that once they are recovered, they will have an easy and non-stressful life — well, lots of people with years of recovery know differently. Normal, straight living is also full of tension and stress.

The Video

Our video today is called "Living with Stress." It shows what stress is, how it affects everyone, and how people use relaxation to deal with stress.

You'll also notice that the stressed-out people in the video don't seem to be using drugs or drinking. Obviously, living clean and sober can also be extremely stressful!

The video is about 23 minutes long, and afterwards we will discuss it and actually try some of the techniques recommended. I hope you enjoy watching the video and find it useful.

What did you think of the video?

Discussion

What are your own signs of stress that you notice in yourself?

Trying out stress-reduction techniques: breathing exercises

Before we start, one of the main things you should focus on is: paying attention to changes in your body. This is extremely important. See if you can notice changes in different parts of your body when we do our relaxation techniques here in a few minutes.

Excessive use of drugs and alcohol actually makes people lose touch with their own bodies. So, in recovery they have to relearn some normal body feelings.

Just think about that — you have to get back in touch with your own body. That is why we are emphasizing the importance of being sensitive to how your body feels.

Let's start some of the breathing exercises. Remember: these exercises are voluntary. We'll start with "breathing for relaxation."

First — proper breathing. Are you a diaphragm breather or a chest breather? Here's how to find out.

Your abdominal diaphragm is just below your bottom ribs. Place your hand on your stomach and see if it goes "in" when you breathe in or out. If it goes in when you breathe air out, good — you are breathing with your abdominal diaphragm.

This is the natural way to relax and breathe; it exchanges a large volume of air with less effort. In fact, it is so natural that newborn babies breathe like this until they grow up and learn the wrong way, which is chest breathing.

If your stomach goes in when you breathe in, you are chest breathing. This is shallow breathing that works harder to replace too little air. It uses the chest and other upper-body muscles. People who yawn a lot during the day may do this.

Let's first practise moving the stomach out to breathe air in.   **Pause.**

It might help to put your hand on your stomach to tell what it is doing.

Now pull your stomach in to breathe out.

OK? Now, here we go with breathing to relax exercises:
1. Relax with your arms in your lap.
2. Slowly breathe in.
3. Hold your breath for a slow count of five.
4. Slowly let your breath out.

Let's do it a few more times.

How did that feel? Did you feel any changes in your body?

Await responses and add any relevant points.

If you feel stress building up, where can you do this relaxed breathing?

Approve of any creative ways to incorporate these techniques into daily life.

Trying out stress-reduction techniques: progressive muscular relaxation

Next we'll learn progressive muscular relaxation. Instead of stretching out on a couch, let's just try it here either stretched out on the mats on the floor or in your chairs, whichever you prefer. Again, this is completely voluntary.

Wait until those who want to stretch out on the floor have done so.

OK, here we go.
1. You would do this technique in a quiet place, with the phone off the hook so you won't be disturbed — possibly with a clock in sight so you can see when the time is up. Undo your belt.
2. Stretch with your **feet** by turning your toes up so that they point more and more at your face.
3. Stretch with your upper **legs** by squeezing them together at the knees.
4. Stretch with your **stomach** by pulling it **in** as much as you can.
5. Stretch with your **stomach** by forcing it **out.**
6. Stretch with your **chest** by expanding it out as much as you can.

7. Do the same with your **shoulders** by shrugging them
    up to your neck.
8. Wait a few seconds and then do the same with the muscles
    in your **lower face;** scrunch them up tight until they feel
    heavy and almost painful: hold for a few seconds and very
    gradually relax them.
9. Last, scrunch up the muscles in your **scalp** as much as you
    can and keep doing that until they feel tight and heavy.
10. Hold the position for a couple of seconds and then very
    gradually relax the tension until the same **scalp** muscles
    are completely relaxed.

Lie quietly for a minute or so before getting up.

Did you feel any changes in your body while you were doing this? **Approve of any positive responses.**

Exercise

Some people prefer other ways to relax. Exercise is one of the
best ways to relax.

Good aerobic exercise drains tension and releases the
endorphins that work against tension in your body.

How often should you exercise? How long should you exercise
each time? There are many opinions about how much exercise
is the right amount for people of different ages and levels of
fitness. Here is just one approach.

A basic rule that is easy to remember goes like this: start
walking fast until you just barely start to sweat. Start timing
yourself with your watch from when you first start to sweat.
Keep walking at a speed just fast enough so that you have
a slight level of sweating for 20 minutes.

Don't push yourself so hard that you are pouring sweat
and become exhausted!

Do this three times each week (or more if you are feeling
particularly stressed out).

Adapting Techniques to Meet Your Needs

Next we're going to discuss taking something — an idea or a technique — and changing it to suit yourself, your recovery and your life.

Think about the relaxation techniques that we just did. In your everyday life, how could you work them in when you need them?

Show approval of any original ways to work these techniques into everyday life.

Have you heard about concentrating on a candle flame to increase your level of calmness?

Here's how to do it:
- Light a candle, sit cross-legged on the floor, and place the candle on the floor.
- Concentrate on the flame for a few seconds, and then close your eyes and try to recreate the image of the flame in your mind. Do this a couple of times.
- You can also try thinking of a special word (perhaps "calm" or "peace") or a helpful phrase (maybe "let go of anger" or "let go of tension" or "feeling safe") or something else important to you.

If you wanted to increase your mental concentration this way, but couldn't use a candle for some reason, how could you do the same thing?

Show approval of any creative answers.

Those are great ideas. Like a lot of things in recovery, you may hear about an idea and then make it work for you by doing it your own way — doing it in a way that suits you. That way you are making it your own.

If there is time, discuss the following example.

For example, a researcher from the Centre for Addiction and Mental Health had an idea. He wanted to achieve a difficult personal goal. So he took a cheap flashlight, a piece of paper, and, in three words, wrote the goal he wanted to achieve. Then he fastened the paper to the flashlight with elastic bands. Each night before he went to bed, he sat in a dark room with the flashlight on, and concentrated on the words, and took 20 slow breaths. Then he switched the flashlight off and tried to re-imagine the glowing image in his mind. He did this three times each night. What do you think happened?

Audiotape

You may have heard about tapes that can help you learn relaxation techniques. Just for a few minutes, let's listen to one.

Play the tape for a few minutes.

Many different tapes like this one are available. Shop around to find one you like. Let's look again at making your own plan for recovery and changing things to suit your needs. For example, if you wanted to use such a tape but you shared a house or apartment with other people, how could you still listen to the tape and learn relaxation?

Someone will likely mention using headphones. Other ideas are: listening to the tape when no one else is around; doing it together with the people you share space with; arranging for the others to give you space to do it alone.

Wrap Up

Now, to wrap up, what did we discover today about relaxation?

Await clients' responses. Show approval for any good ideas. Add the following points if they are not covered:

We may also have discovered the following:
a) Heavy stress can be part of life even for people who have been clean and sober for years.
b) Relaxation techniques can make a difference in how well you deal with stress.
c) You can not only alter relaxation techniques to suit what you want to do, but you can also adapt other ideas on recovery to suit your daily life.
d) You can do some actual relaxation techniques for yourself.

INTRODUCTION
TO RECOVERY

Spirituality

SPIRITUALITY

FACILITATOR'S CHECKLIST AND INFORMATION

Before you start, check that you have the following:

- overheads
    1. AA, NA and CA are spiritual, but not religious
    2. Differences between Religion and Spirituality
    3. A Spiritual Kindergarten
    4. Madonna song "...living in a material world"
    5. What is spirituality?
    6. To see spirituality in…
    7. To see spirituality in…
    8. Recovery and Spirituality

Audio/Visual Requirements

- overhead projector and projection screen
- whiteboard and markers

Purpose of the Module

to introduce group members to basic concepts of spirituality

Objectives

1. to provide information on the benefits of spiritual aspects of recovery
2. to promote participation in this module as a way of beginning to think about spirituality and how it relates to life in recovery
3. to encourage and support clients sharing their experiences, thoughts and attitudes about spirituality
4. to understand the differences between spirituality and religion

Special Considerations

- If a client complains about the topic, emphasize that this is not a complaint session. Explain that we want to encourage people to gain new knowledge.
- Some clients may have had bad experiences with religion or may attribute some of their problems to religious factors. If a client states these concerns, validate them and explain that all of our experiences make up our "spiritual self." Add that by participating in today's group, it is hoped that clients will better understand their past negative experiences.
- Be aware of your own biases and be willing to present the material in an objective yet confident manner.

NOTE: The facilitator's script and other material to be covered in the group session is in plain text. Instructions for facilitators are presented in **Bold** text.

Getting Started
Each time you start the group, review the following:

Group Norms
• Arrive on time.
• No food or drink is allowed during group sessions.
• Group members will sit in a semi-circle around the whiteboard.
• With the exception of washroom breaks, anyone who wishes to leave the group must first ask the facilitator's permission.
• Any feedback to other members is limited to how you relate to what has been said. Please do not give any advice or make judgmental comments.
• Only one person may speak at a time.
• Any other suggestions for today's group?   **Ask participants.**

How is everyone today?   **Ask around the circle.**

Does anyone have any issues that they wish to raise regarding the Detox Centre?

Introduction

The main purpose of the Introduction to Recovery Group is to exchange information that will help you make informed lifestyle changes and orient you to group in preparation for ongoing treatment.

The purpose of this session, Spirituality, is to discuss spirituality and how it relates to recovery from addictions and societal norms. Many people view spirituality as an important part of recovery.

Today we'll look at the following areas:
• what spirituality is and isn't
• the difference between spirituality and religion
• why so many people involved in recovery consider spirituality to be an important part of that journey.

The Session

A few points about group today:

To begin with, usually in group we ask someone what they think about a particular topic. But today, because our topic of spirituality is such a personal and private part of yourself, we'll wait for people to speak up on their own accord. I won't ask anyone to say something. So, if you would like to say something, please speak up!

I hope many of you will participate today.

Second, if anyone has real problems even with the topic of spirituality, please keep an open mind and at least listen to what we have to say. Some people use religion and spirituality as a way to show that they are better than others. Let's not do that here today. Let's make a rule of "no personal comparisons." That's a good rule for group anyway, and it is especially good for today's topic.

We designed this group today so that anyone, even a confirmed atheist, should have no problems with it. Our group today is not about telling you what you should do. It is about discussing what other people have to say about spirituality and recovery.

(You may want to explain the terms "atheist" and "agnostic.")

Here's a promise: we won't try to convince you to accept or reject any part of spirituality. We'll only tell you what other people have said about it.

Why are we taking a whole group session to discuss spirituality? Because almost everyone in addiction treatment views working on spirituality — however you may see that — as important to recovery.

Please notice that I said, "spirituality — however you may see it," because choosing your own concept or concepts of spirituality is a solid and time-tested approach in treatment and recovery. Atheists and agnostics were among the earliest members of AA. They helped Bill W. and Dr. Bob as they started up AA, and they pushed for this approach to spirituality.

So, the earliest ideas in AA were set up so that even people who hated religion would still be comfortable with this kind of help for their sobriety and would want to remain in the group. And we know that thousands of atheists and agnostics have been comfortable with and have been participating, useful members of AA and other 12-step groups. Some people have also gone from working on their own spirituality to finding their way to religion.

You probably noticed that I mentioned religion and spirituality. Let's first look at how these concepts differ.

Show overhead 1 (AA, NA and CA are spiritual, but not religious).

What are your thoughts about this statement? What are your ideas on the difference between religion and spirituality in 12-step programs?

Summarize good ideas on the whiteboard. (Leave some space on the whiteboard for later.)

If someone is hostile or heavily negative, say "I'm sure you've got good reasons for saying that, and many people have felt the same at some time. Let's see what others think." You can say: "Many people in these groups do not support any church or religion," or "The founders of 12-step groups were opposed to linking sobriety with any religion. They still reject any such link." Or ask: "Can anyone give examples of how 12-step groups like AA and NA separate religion and spirituality?"

Here's a couple of ways to look at these differences.

Show overhead 2 (Differences between Religion and Spirituality).

Do you see the differences between religion and spirituality here?

Religion is more about an organized group of worshippers, while spirituality can be one person's search for meaning and feeling connected to the world of nature. Spirituality can also involve several people searching together for a link to something bigger than themselves.

What is the difference between a "higher deity" and a "higher power"?

Good answers here could be:
- **A higher deity is usually defined and assigned by someone else, such as a religious leader.**
- **A higher power is one you choose based on what is important to you.**

Just so we know that we understand these words, what are some examples of:
- religious rules (what you can and can't do)
- religious roles (a function or position in a group)
- religious rituals (ceremonies that are carried out with the worshippers attending)
- relationships and their meaning for you (ties of caring and affection between people)

Here are the words of Bill W. on this topic. Here he is discussing AA's history.

Show overhead 3 (A Spiritual Kindergarten). Read the first quotation.

Then he talks about the debate in the very first AA meetings over whether to make "God" a part of AA belief. As a group they decided to leave out "God" and "religion" and to offer spirituality instead. Bill W. then says:

Read second quotation on overhead 3.

See how modest their goals are? And how they left the door open for most people to feel comfortable in the group?

Now here's another way to look at spirituality, but from the opposite view.

What does Madonna mean by "the material world"? What does it mean to you? Something different?

Did any of you ever feel that you were just living in the material world? How did it feel?

Wait for their answers and comment if you wish.

Did life get better for you? How did it improve?

Discuss their answers.

Next we'll look at a couple of ways in which people escape from just "living in the material world."

Show overhead 5 (What is spirituality?).

Have any of you asked yourself these questions? What do you think about these issues? How does working them through help recovery?

Discuss the responses.

Next we'll look at how you can tell when you are connected to the spiritual side of your life. One way to know is when you feel good when something very special and good happens to you. This good feeling about the world and yourself is a large part of what we mean by "spirituality."

Show overhead 6 (To see spirituality in...) and discuss what it feels like to have these special things happen to you — to receive a hug from a child or a letter from a friend, or to be in a beautiful and special place.

By now, we hope you can see that none of the things we are saying about spirituality is "for addicts only." Spirituality is for everyone. This module could be presented anywhere — such as in schools or in youth or adult classes.

This topic is like many other topics in group because everyone — straight or not, young or old, rich or poor — still needs to work on things like wellness, nutrition and relaxation techniques.

Would you believe that I still need to work on these areas?

If you wish to, discuss how you, just like everyone else, need to work at eating right, keeping healthy, getting enough sleep, watching for and handling denial, and getting enough relaxation time.

How do you know when you are doing well with these things? We suggest that you check how you feel in your body as well as your mind when you are safe and healthy. And work hard to keep yourself feeling safe and healthy.

Here's a good test that anyone, straight and sober or not, can use to tell if what they are doing is right for them, if it's right for their health and how they feel about themselves. It's an easy test — just take a good look in the mirror!

If something makes you feel bad about yourself, or is bad for your health, you'll see it in the way you look! This self-test is from Bill W.

Show overhead 7 (To see spirituality in…).

Here are some of the ways that people come to feel better about themselves through spirituality.

"Finding meaning and purpose in life" — how does that help a normal someone in his or her daily life?

Our last overhead today looks at how working on spirituality can help people move from negative feelings to more positive ones.

Wrap Up

What did we discover today about spirituality?

Discuss their responses. Summarize any good answers in one or two words. Add the following points if they are not covered:

We also may have learned about:
1. Why there is agreement among people in addictions treatment that working on your spirituality is crucial to recovery.
2. The differences between religion and spirituality.
3. Sensing good spirituality because it helps you: to feel that your life has meaning, to feel good about yourself and others, to feel connected to other people and to nature, and to feel safe and healthy.

We know that some people have problems with spirituality. If you have had problems in this area, how do you feel now?

Respond as appropriate.

"AA, NA and CA are spiritual, but not religious."

What does this statement mean?

Differences between Religion and Spirituality

Religion

A formal, organized group, with the worship of one or more higher deities

Rules, **R**oles, and **R**ituals

Spirituality

Individual seeking for personal values, for meaning in our lives, and for meaning of events in our lives

R*elationships: their quality, and what they mean to you*

Adapted from: Joachim, Kitty. (1988). *Spirituality and Chemical Dependency: Guidelines for Treatment:* Oxford MI: The Oxford Institute.

A Spiritual Kindergarten

"We are only operating a spiritual kindergarten in which people are enabled to get over drinking and…go on living to better effect."

"Every voice was playing its appointed part. Our atheists and agnostics widened our gateway so that all who suffer might pass through, regardless of their belief or lack of belief."

Adapted from: Bill W. (1984). *As Bill Sees It: The AA Way of Life ... Selected Writings of AA's Co-founder.*

...We are living

in a material world

Thanks to: Madonna

What is spirituality?

Spirituality is the search for answers to the following questions:

"Who am I?"

"What is the purpose of my life?"

"If all signs of material life die and disappear, what is the value of my own life?"

Adapted from: Baker, T. (n.d.) *Understanding the Spiritual Nature of Addiction.*

To see spirituality in...

1. That special, wonderful "Ah" feeling when:

- a child hugs you

- you receive an unexpected letter from a friend, or

- you see a beautiful sunset or enjoy a quiet park or nature area.

Adapted from: Harrison, J & Burnard, P. (1993). *Spirituality and Nursing Practice*.

To see spirituality in...

2. Some of these ways of thinking:

  • finding meaning and purpose in life

  • trusting yourself and others

  • love for yourself and others

  • hope

  • forgiveness

  • for some people, a relationship with
    a higher power.

Adapted from: Harrison, J & Burnard, P. (1993). *Spirituality and Nursing Practice*.

Recovery and Spirituality

Moving from:

Fear	→ to →	Trust
Self-pity	→ to →	Gratitude
Resentment	→ to →	Acceptance
Dishonesty	→ to →	Honesty
Guilt	→ to →	Forgiveness
Despair	→ to →	Hope

Adapted from Joachim, Kitty. (1988) *Spirituality and Chemical Dependency: Guidelines for Treatment.* Oxford MI: The Oxford Institute.

INTRODUCTION
TO RECOVERY

Continuing Care

CONTINUING CARE

FACILITATOR'S CHECKLIST AND INFORMATION

Before you start, check that you have the following:

- overheads
  1. The Addictions Continuum
  2. Specific Types of Programs in the Addictions Continuum
  3. Sample Admission Criteria: Withdrawal Management Centres
  4. Sample Admission Criteria: Outpatient Programs
  5. Sample Admission Criteria: Residential Treatment
  6. General Social Services (2)
- handouts entitled "Assistance in the Community" and pencils for every group member

Audio/Visual Requirements

- overhead projector and projection screen
- whiteboard and markers

Purpose of the Module

to offer assurance that a variety of services are available in the community to care for the needs (physical, social, economic and spiritual) of people in recovery and to provide knowledge of what general services are available and how they may be accessed

Objectives

1. to help clients begin thinking about how they will choose the types of services they will need to access.
2. to help clients understand that they will need to qualify for entrance to other programs, and how they will qualify.
3. to encourage and support sharing with others around this topic.

Special Considerations

- Some clients may have considerable experience in the various components of the addictions and social services continuum. However, much of their experience may have been negative. Consequently, you may wish to acknowledge the system's shortcomings at the beginning of the session, rather than having to address them while you are presenting positive information.

NOTE: The facilitator's script and other material to be covered in the group session is in plain text. Instructions for facilitators are presented in **Bold** text.

Getting Started
Each time you start the group, review the following:

Group Norms
• Arrive on time.
• No food or drink is allowed during group sessions.
• Group members will sit in a semi-circle around the whiteboard.
• With the exception of washroom breaks, anyone who wishes to leave the group must first ask the facilitator's permission.
• Any feedback to other members is limited to how you relate to what has been said. Please do not give any advice or make judgmental comments.
• Only one person may speak at a time.
• Any other suggestions for today's group?   **Ask participants.**

How is everyone today?   **Ask around the circle.**

Does anyone have any issues that they wish to raise regarding the Detox Centre?

Introduction

The main purpose of the Introduction to Recovery Group is to exchange information that will help you make informed lifestyle changes and orient you to group in preparation for ongoing treatment.

This session, Continuing Care, addresses the types of help that are available for you in the early stage of recovery and explains how to access them.

The Session

Our goals today are:

1. to understand what types of services are available for people in recovery

2. to identify the differences among these services so that you can start thinking about which ones will be appropriate for you

3. to learn to think about how you will qualify for the services that you want to access

4. to hear what other people here have to say about their recovery plans in case they have some good ideas that can help you.

The first thing we'll do today is fill out one of these forms to help us think about what services we will need if we are going to continue in recovery.

Distribute the handouts "Assistance in the Community" and pencils to all group members.

In the space provided, write in which services you think you will need in order to continue your recovery.

Now let's go around the circle and discuss what you wrote down. Who would like to start?

Now let's take an overview — the big picture of what is out there for people recovering from an addiction.

When you work every day with people who are starting their recovery, you become familiar with two systems of services.

First, there are services that are designed especially for people with addictions. What are some examples of these?

The second system of services that you will likely need are for general social services — those services that anyone who needs help can access. What are a few types of general social services?

Why do we go to treatment at all? Why don't we just walk out of here and simply stay clean and sober?

If you want and need treatment, how do you decide which treatment program is right for you?

Once you decide, how do you get into the program you want?

You have to meet the program's matching criteria; in other words, there is no sense in attending a treatment program that does not meet your needs. Some of your needs include the following:
• how long you've been clean or dry
• your desire and motivation to make lifestyle changes
• the amount of support you have
• whether you can meet the qualifications for admission to some programs
• what services the programs offer.

What are some of the problems you might face getting into the treatment program you want?

• not being clean or sober long enough
• not having a safe living situation or enough support
  from people to help you in your recovery
• not enough space in the program
• not meeting the program's admission criteria

Please note that all six components can be connected
to the 12 steps.

Also note that it is possible to go back and forth within each
component. There are two main reasons for this:
1. The type of treatment you enter may be inappropriate so you
   may need to adjust your goal (i.e., you may try outpatient
   treatment and discover you need more support). This is
   known as a stepped-care model (where you receive the least
   intrusive level of care to start with).
2. There should be flexibility regarding relapse (i.e., if someone
   relapses while in any component of care, he or she may need
   to be referred to detox or reassessed).

This overhead breaks down the continuum to specific target
groups. Not all of these are available in every community.

Can anyone identify some specific programs that match the
various types? For example, does anyone know if youth
programs are offered here in our community?

Now let's look at some general admission criteria.

So far we've discussed one kind of service for people in
recovery: treatment programs.

Next, let's take a look at the big picture — what is available
besides support from the addictions system.

Do you remember earlier that I mentioned that social services
are there for everyone — those who don't have substance use
problems as well as those who do? Let's look more closely at
some of these general social services.

The overhead is a list of general social services offered in most communities. As with the addictions services, it may vary. Can anyone share any positive experiences related to any of these services?

Wrap Up

What did we discover today about the types of continuing care available for those working on their recovery?

Here's a way to check if you learned anything new today. Look again at the handout that you filled in earlier (Assistance in the Community) and see if you would fill in more kinds of assistance now.

See how much more aware you are now? What are some of the new items you added?

Great, that's it for today. We hope we hear real success stories from those of you who end up accessing some of the services we discussed today.

The Addictions Continuum

Assessment & Referral		Detox Centres

Outpatient:		Residential:
• Day Programs • Weekly Programs • Individualized		• Short Term • Long Term

Recovery Homes		Continuing Care

Self Help

NOTE: Entry into the Continuum can occur at any point other than Continuing Care. However, the main points of entry are Detox and Assessment/Referral Centres.

Specific Types of Programs in the Addictions Continuum

1 withdrawal management and detoxification

2 assessment, stabilization and treatment planning

3 counselling:

   a) weekly counselling for one to three
      times per week

   b) daily counselling for five days per week

4 day programs for youth

5 family support

6 residences (or) residential treatment for:

   - men and young men
   - seniors
   - women and young women
   - young offenders
   - youth only

7 aftercare

Sample Admission Criteria

Withdrawal Management Centres

- intoxicated or in withdrawal

- needs 24-hour monitoring of withdrawal symptoms

- does not need immediate medical care

- appropriate behaviour (e.g., non-violent)

- medications are appropriate (e.g., non-addictive)

Adapted from: Health Recovery Steering Committee. (1997). Admission Discharge Criteria.

Sample Admission Criteria

Outpatient Programs

- substance-free or appropriately limited use for the type of treatment

- no medical psychiatric issues that will interfere with treatment

- assessment indicated a need to learn problem-solving and/or general life skills

- is committed to treatment goals

- assessment indicates moderate dependence

- is in appropriate living environment

- able to meet scheduled appointments

Adapted from: Health Recovery Steering Committee. (1997). Admission Discharge Criteria.

OVERHEAD 4

Sample Admission Criteria

Residential Treatment

- has been and remains abstinent for appropriate length of time (depending on substance)

- does not require a medically monitored approach to treatment

- committed to treatment goals

- assessment indicates severe dependence

- needs 24-hour access to support environment

- barriers to treatment are resolved

Adapted from: Health Recovery Steering Committee. (1997). Admission Discharge Criteria.

General Social Services 1
(not listed in order of importance)

1 Social Assistance
EXAMPLE: a social worker or case worker for welfare or other forms of assistance, and to co-ordinate other services listed below

2 Financial Counselling
EXAMPLE: to settle outstanding debts

3 Mental Health Clinic
EXAMPLE: to deal with sexual abuse issues

4 Parenting Classes
EXAMPLE: parenting skills to be a better father or mother to your children, and to help get access to your children

5 Education (literacy, high school diploma, vocational counselling, trades courses, community colleges, university) for part-time or full-time study
EXAMPLES: high school equivalent diploma; certificate program in finances, computers, landscaping; any trade or profession; a university degree

General Social Services 2

6 Housing/Shelter

7 Recreation

EXAMPLE: to become active in your spare time (sports, hobbies, other activities that make you feel good and don't involve substance use)

8 Legal Services

EXAMPLES: John Howard Society, Elizabeth Fry Society, legal aid

9 Self-Improvement Classes

EXAMPLES: assertiveness training, anger management training, relaxation and stress reduction classes, communication skills

Assistance in the Community

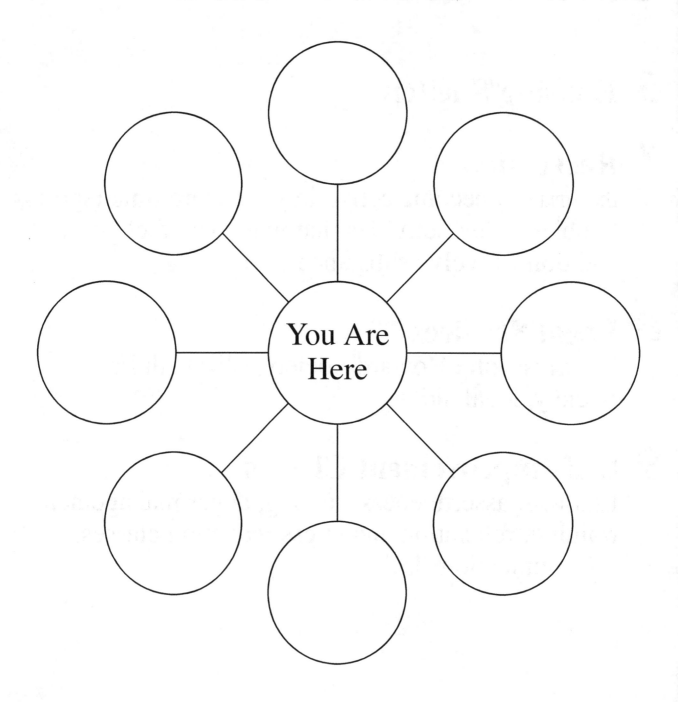

You Are
Here

INTRODUCTION
TO RECOVERY

Denial

DENIAL

FACILITATOR'S CHECKLIST AND INFORMATION

Before you start, check that you have the following:	• overheads
	    1. Scarlett O'Hara quotation
	    2. Layers of Denial
	    3. Examples of Denial in Everyday Life and Addiction

Audio/Visual Requirements	• overhead projector and projection screen • whiteboard and markers
Purpose of the Module	to provide an overview of the concept of denial and its role in normal daily life — both for non-addicted people as well as for those in recovery from addictions
Objectives	1. to define denial 2. to encourage and support sharing about denial and its role in their lives, as well as in the lives of people who don't have an addiction
Special Considerations	• Some group members may think of the subject of denial as accusatory in nature or may view the subject as unnecessary. Validate their perception but also point out the importance of understanding the process of denial.

NOTE: The facilitator's script and other material to be covered in the group session is in plain text. Instructions for facilitators are presented in **Bold** text.

Getting Started

Each time you start the group, review the following:

Group Norms
- Arrive on time.
- No food or drink is allowed during group sessions.
- Group members will sit in a semi-circle around the whiteboard.
- With the exception of washroom breaks, anyone who wishes to leave the group must first ask the facilitator's permission.
- Any feedback to other members is limited to how you relate to what has been said. Please do not give any advice or make judgmental comments.
- Only one person may speak at a time.
- Any other suggestions for today's group?   **Ask participants.**

How is everyone today?   **Ask around the circle.**

Does anyone have any issues that they wish to raise regarding the Detox Centre?

Introduction

The main purpose of the Introduction to Recovery Group is to exchange information that will help you make informed lifestyle changes and orient you to group in preparation for ongoing treatment.

The purpose of this session, Denial, is to discuss this concept as it relates to everyday daily life and how it relates to addiction.

The Session

Has anyone here heard the word "denial" before? In what context was it used?

Encourage clients to share their experiences.

Today we'll look at what denial is and how denial works in everyday life for everybody — whether straight or using, sober or addicted, young, middle-aged or old.

Everyone uses denial at some time or other. It's just that some people use it only every now and again, and usually for small things in life, while others deny basic problems of self-abuse and inflict severe harm on themselves and on others.

First, let's talk about denial as it is used by everyone.

Here are some examples:
- When people hear about any horrible or shocking news, their first response is usually to say, "No! It can't be true!" or "I don't believe it." A recent example occurred when Princess Diana was killed. Most people initially reacted by saying, "No! It must be a mistake."
- When things start to wear out and we put off replacing them. For example, we say to ourselves, "My winter coat will get through another season." But a few months later the coat starts to fall apart.
- When problems occurs in relationships or friendships, we often think it is just a temporary setback and link it to some other cause.
- When we are tired, run down, and our energy is low, we tell ourselves that we'll "catch up on the weekend."

These are some examples of everyday denial. So, what's happening in these cases?

People look for protection from the harsh facts that make them feel at risk so they deny that there is a problem. Remember that, in the following cases, it's normal to protect yourself and to buy yourself some time by denying that there is a problem:
- when sudden death happens to someone you know
- when you are short of cash and you need new clothes

• when a friendship or relationship has problems and is at risk
• when your health or level of energy is getting low and you
  could become sick.

People who study denial in everyday life feel that it is a
way to buy some time to deal with a problem later rather
than immediately.

**Show overhead 1 (Scarlett O'Hara
quotation).**

Just like Scarlett O'Hara, most of the time we can think about
and deal with the small things tomorrow. This kind of denial
buys us some time and often lets us make a better plan than
if we rushed out to take care of everything as soon as it looked
like a problem.

Can you think of times when you used denial to deal with
a small problem?

But denying basic problems has some effects. Let's look
at these negative effects.

We'll look at the layers of denial we build, and how they
keep us from taking care of a problem.

"Facts" refers to denying basic facts that anyone else can see.
An example here would be when someone says, "I don't have
a problem," when everyone else can see that they do have
a problem. Can anyone here share examples of that in your
own lives?

"Implications" refers to admitting to the facts, but denying that
they imply that you have a problem. Examples could include
saying:
• "Yeah, I drink a lot and got arrested a couple of times for
  driving that way, but I've never hurt anyone, so it's OK."
• "Yeah, sure I shoot up, but only with people who I know
  don't have AIDS, hepatitis or other diseases. I wouldn't
  inject with just anybody."
• "Sure, I drink several nights each week, but I hold it well
  and I still do great on my job."

Someone in this phase admits to the facts of addiction,
admits the implication that they are addicted, but denies
the need to change.
For example someone might say:
• "Yeah, I've lost a couple of jobs now, and I can't stop
  using, but it's gonna be OK."

Or the person denies responsibility to change. An example could
be saying:
• "So I'm drinking too much, but you can't hold that hit-and-run
  against me. I was drunk!"

Or the person denies that he or she can change. For example
someone might say:
• "I know I'm an addict, but I tried a couple of times to kick it.
  But, well, something always happened."

After you knew you were addicted, did any of you deny your
need to change?

Did anyone here ever deny his or her responsibility to get clean?

Did anyone deny that he or she could change?

Denial of feelings is different from the previous stages because
the user doesn't know that he or she is doing it. The user is
unaware of shutting off feelings and painful memories. But in
recovery these feelings begin to come out with a lot of pain,
shame and guilt. And these painful feelings can make someone
desperate for their drug or a drink, and they may relapse.

That's why a good support group is important — you never
know what time of day or night those memories of shame and
guilt will surface and overwhelm you. And when they do, you'll
need someone to talk to.

And at the centre of all of those layers...

YOU — your real inner self is hidden away here.

Do you see why people talk about the "layers of denial"?

Now that we've gone over the basics of the layers of denial, let's see how they compare for all of us — straight and sober, as well as addicted.

Show overhead 3 (Examples of Denial in Everyday Life and Addiction). Uncover only the first two rows: 1) "On the Job," "With Partner" and "With an Addiction," and 2) "Denial of Facts." Cover the rest of the rows.

Let's look at "Denial of Facts."

Next, there's "Denial of Implications."

Wrap Up

What did we discover today about denial?

We also may have discovered that denial is:
• something that everyone does
• a way to deal with problems in life
• a major block to self-growth if it is part of an addiction.

"I'll think about that tomorrow."

(Scarlett O'Hara in *Gone With the Wind*)

Adapted from: Kearney, R. (1996). *Within the Wall of Denial: Conquering Addictive Behaviors*.

Layers of Denial

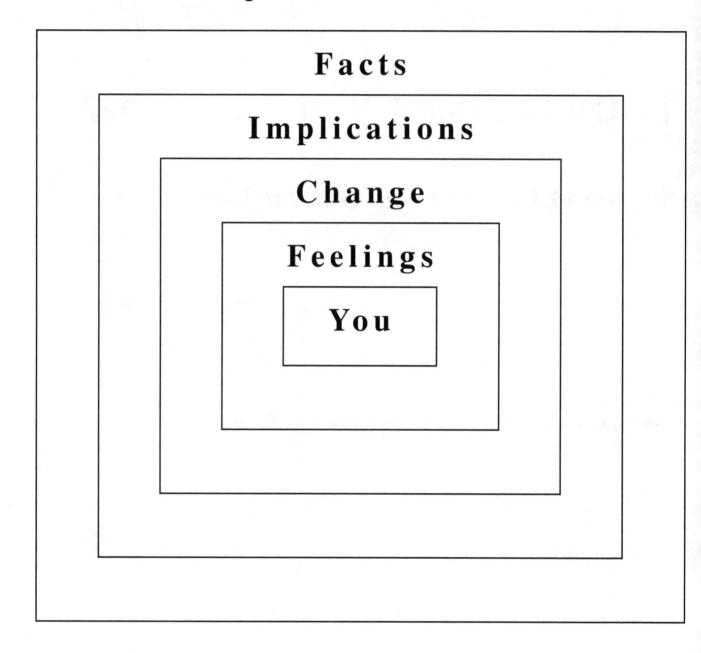

Adapted from: Kearney, R. (1996). *Within the Wall of Denial: Conquering Addictive Behaviors.*

Examples of Denial in Everyday Life and Addiction

	ON THE JOB *Example:* **Often Late for Work**	**WITH PARTNER** *Example:* **Increasingly Serious Verbal Fights**	**WITH AN ADDICTION**
DENIAL OF FACTS	"Everybody's late sometimes. I'm not late any more than anyone else."	"It's good, it's OK, we're just clearing the air."	"I've only (drank or used) too much just a couple of times."
DENIAL OF IMPLICATIONS	"Anyway, I get more work done than those nerds who are always on time."	"I know [she or he] still feels the same about me – I can tell."	"I'll give you a long list of people who drink/use more than I do!"
DENIAL OF CHANGE	"I've only been late a couple of times."	"When my job gets better, then there won't be so much tension between us, OK?"	"Why are you making so much of it – I was drunk!"
DENIAL OF FEELINGS	"I'm OK, it doesn't bother me."	"I'm OK, it doesn't bother me."	"I'm OK, it doesn't bother me."

Adapted from: Kearney, R. (1996). *Within the Wall of Denial: Conquering Addictive Behaviors.*

INTRODUCTION
TO RECOVERY

References

REFERENCES

Addiction Research Foundation. (1992). *Progressive Muscular Relaxation* (Cassette Recording No. ARF 5001). Toronto: Addiction Research Foundation.

Alcoholics Anonymous. (1976). *Alcoholics Anonymous* (3rd ed.). New York: Alcoholics Anonymous World Services Inc.

Alcoholics Anonymous. (1977*). Alcoholics Anonymous Comes of Age: A Brief History of AA*. New York: Alcoholics Anonymous World Services Inc.

Baker, T. (n.d.). *Understanding the Spiritual Nature of Addiction: A Guide for Clergy and Laypersons Concerned About the Nature, Diagnosis, and Treatment of Addictive Disorders*. Providence, RI: Manisses Communications Group, Inc.

Beasley, J. & Knightly, S. (1993). *Food for Recovery: The Complete Nutritional Companion for Recovering from Alcoholism, Drug Addiction, and Eating Disorders*. New York: Crown Trade Paperbacks.

Biery, J.R., Williford, J.H. & McMullen, E.A. (1991). Alcohol craving in rehabilitation: assessment of nutrition therapy. *Journal of the American Dietetic Association, 9 (4)*, 463–466.

British Columbia Ministry of Health. (1992). *Choosing Wellness* (pamphlet). Vancouver: British Columbia Ministry of Health.

Canadian Dietetic Association. (1993). *Nutrition Checkup for Women* (fact sheet).

Coren, S. (1996). *Sleep Thieves*. New York: Free Press Paperbacks/Simon & Schuster.

Daniel, E. (1991). Nutritional implications in recovery from substance abuse. *Employee Assistance Quarterly, 7 (1)*, 1–7.

Davis, A. (1970). *Let's Eat Right to Keep Fit*. New York: Harcourt Brace Jovanovich, Inc.

Dotto, L. (1990). *Asleep In the Fast Lane: The Impact of Sleep on Work*. Toronto: Stoddart Publishing Co. Ltd.

Fernstrom, J. (1994). Dietary amino acids and brain function. *Journal of the American Dietetic Association, 94 (1)*, 71–77.

Finnegan, J. & Gray, D. (1990). *Recovery From Addiction: A Comprehensive Understanding of Substance Abuse with Nutritional Therapies for Recovering Addicts and Co-Dependents*. Berkeley, CA: Celestial Arts.

Harrison, J. & Burnard, P. (1993). *Spirituality and Nursing Practice*. Brookfield, VT: Ashgate Publishing Company.

Health Recovery Steering Committee. (1997). Admission Discharge Criteria Subcommittee, reporting to the Ontario Substance Abuse Bureau. Toronto: Queen's Park.

Joachim, K. (1998). *Spirituality and Chemical Dependency: Guidelines for Treatment*. Oxford, MI: The Oxford Institute.

Kearney, R. (1996). *Within the Wall of Denial: Conquering Addictive Behaviors*. New York: W.W. Norton & Company.

Ketcham, K. & Mueller, L. (1983). *Eating Right to Stay Sober*. Seattle, WA: Madrona Publishers.

Kort, M. & Smith, S. (1993). *Stop Smoking Program: Facilitators' Guide*. Toronto: Addiction Research Foundation.

Larson, J. (1992). *Alcoholism — The Biochemical Connection*. New York: Villard Books.

Marsano, L. (1993). Alcohol and malnutrition. *Alcohol Health & Research World, 17 (14)*, 284-291.

Milk Marketing Board. (1990). Fact Sheets.

Mish, F. (Ed.). (1985). *Webster's Ninth New International Dictionary*. Springfield, MA: Merriam-Webster Inc.

Prochaska, J., DiClemente, C. & Norcross, J. (1992). In search of how people change: Applications to addictive behaviors. *American Psychologist, 47 (9),* 1102-1114.

Rees, A. & Willey, C. (Eds.). (1993). *Personal Health Reporter*. Washington, DC: Gale Research Inc.

Shulman, L. (1979). *The Skills of Helping Individuals and Groups*. Itasca, IL: F.E. Peacock Publishers, Inc.

W., Bill. (1984). *As Bill Sees It: The AA Way of Life ... Selected Writings of AA's Co-Founder*. New York: Alcoholics Anonymous World Services Inc.

W., Bill. (1996). *Twleve Steps and Twelve Traditions*. New York: Alcoholics Anonymous World Services Inc.

Wesson, D. (Consensus Panel Chair). (1995). *Detoxification From Alcohol and Other Drugs* (Treatment Improvement Protocol Tip Series #19). Rockville, MD: U.S. Department of Health and Human Services.

Appendix A:
Videos Screened at 501

APPENDIX A:

VIDEOS SCREENED AT 501

The videos listed below are an additional resource that could be used to help facilitate effective early recovery groups. Depending on your client population and the functional aspects of your program, videos could be used in conjunction with the material in the modules or as a substitute for the material. In some cases, depending on your client group, you may determine that a video followed by a discussion on its contents is a more effective means of presenting material to your group. If you were to use a video in conjunction with the module material (depending on time), you may wish to present the module material one day and follow it up with a relevant video to the material later in the day or the next day.

However, as stated previously in the manual, we have found that to use videos alone on a regular basis does not promote the level of group interaction that is required in order for early recovery clients to enjoy and learn from group.

THE ADDICTED BRAIN   (1987; 26 min.)
Cost: $149.00 (US)
Available from Kinetic
(ARF Library # 960)
AUDIENCE: *Adults, health professionals, university students*
SYNOPSIS: "Each brain is a kind of pharmacist," this video asserts. "Drugs go with the territory of being human," whether dispensed by the brain as a normal function (often in response to specific activities) or consumed in an effort to alter a mood. Effects on the brain of alcohol and other drugs are described. Addiction to activities are also discussed. "Runner's high," the result of increased endorphin production during extended high-aerobic activity, is given as an example. Other addictions, it says, can include high-risk lifestyles, which can influence brain chemistry. Any activity that produces rewards in the brain has the potential for addiction.

ADDICTION AND THE FAMILY   (1986; 19 min.)
Cost: $100.00 (US)
Available from Kinetic
(ARF Library #2122)
AUDIENCE: *General, families*

SYNOPSIS: This program illustrates a variety of issues that develop in families where one or more members have substance abuse problems. Focusing on the "G" family, the place of environment and heredity are discussed. In addition, family members remember the violence, shame, fear and responsibility they felt. Through recovery they learned that they can't control it, can't fix it, and it's not their fault. Interviews with experts conclude the program with the commentaries on how ACOAs cope, problems in treatment and how to get help.

BROTHER EARL: STREET TALK   (1989; 60 min.)
Cost: $295.00
Available from Kinetic
(ARF Library # 1089.1)
AUDIENCE: *People with drug or alcohol problems, African-Americans*
SYNOPSIS: Brother Earl uses a flip chart and a folksy, preacher-style delivery to describe the process of addiction, in a videotaped lecture format. He discusses the concepts of tolerance, avoidance of family, work and money problems ("to finance your habit, you walk out of the house with Grandma's TV with her teeth still on top of it") and physical deterioration. Brother

Earl encourages his audience, comprising drug users and those in recovery, to share their experiences and to role-play some of the concepts discussed.

BROTHER EARL: WHAT PROBLEM?
(1989; 60 min.)
Cost: $295.00
Available from Kinetic
(ARF Library #1089.2)
AUDIENCE: *People in recovery, African-Americans*
SYNOPSIS: Brother Earl continues his humorous and affable approach in discussing denial: "When we talk about denial, doesn't it sound a bit like lying?" He works with his audience and suggests that denial is a natural process similar to the process of grief: "When you gave up your drug, you gave up something that may have been closer to you than your child or your job." Group members give examples from their lives, and Brother Earl concludes with "what we can do about it."

COMEBACKER: THE BOB WELCH STORY
(1981; 22 min.)
Cost: $295.00
Available from Kinetic
(ARF Library #470)
SYNOPSIS: Bob Welch, playing baseball for the Los Angeles Dodgers in 1978, won a World Series game. However, Bob Welch is an alcoholic. Bob feels that his problems started when he was 16 years old. He felt afraid of girls and drank before going to parties to gain some courage; he drank in college to get drunk because then he did not feel that anyone liked him. When he joined the Dodgers, he felt that he was liked only because of his skill as a pitcher and he drank to mask his feelings. One day he came to a game drunk and made such a scene he was confronted by the Dodgers' management. Don Newcombe of the Dodgers' organization, himself an alcoholic, convinced Bob to go to a rehabilitation centre. Bob recognizes that his drinking is a problem and now is enjoying life sober.

FATHER MARTIN: GUIDELINES   (1977; 48 min.)
Cost: $225.00 (US)
Available from FMS Productions
(ARF Library # 254)
AUDIENCE: *Adults, AA, detox clients*
SYNOPSIS: Father Martin is addressing a large audience about eight guidelines in working with alcoholics. He urges people who wish to help alcoholics to be aware of their own attitudes, learn to recognize and know what being addicted to alcohol means, and to make alcoholics responsible for their own behaviour. Father Martin also urges the audience not to "go it alone," but to use community resources and not become discouraged. His talk is punctuated with humorous anecdotes and jokes to emphasize his points.

THE HONOR OF ALL   (1986; Part I)
Cost: $149.00
Available from Canadian Learning Centre
(ARF Library #2038)
AUDIENCE: *Native people, general*
SYNOPSIS: In 1971; Phyllis Chelsea took a stand against alcohol. Five days after she quit drinking, Andy, her husband did the same. For the first two years, Phyllis and Andy were the only sober members of the band. After Andy was elected chief, visible changes bean to appear. Between 1971 and 1986 the Alkalai Lake Band turned their lives around to achieve a sobriety rate of 95 per cent.

A MATTER OF BALANCE   (1988; 23 min.)
Cost: $595.00
Available from Kinetic
(ARF Library # 846)
AUDIENCE: *12 years +*
SYNOPSIS: Our central nervous system's efforts to keep our bodies balanced are illustrated in the film by a tight-rope walker. If we take any kind of drug it can upset the balance and cause problems. The effects of stimulants, depressants and hallucinogens are shown, and users describe their experiences with these drugs.

THE PLAN: ADDICTIONS-HIV (1992; 38 min.)
Cost: $312.00
Available from Canadian Learning Centre
(ARF Library #1093)

AUDIENCE: *HIV-positive drug users, health professionals, students*

SYNOPSIS: Robert and Eileen are recovered addicts: they are also HIV positive. Through interviews, they describe how they have dealt with both their substance abuse and HIV. Experts discuss relevant issues; for example, how staying clean can improve immune response in HIV-positive clients. The video addresses concepts such as self-destruction, denial, medical awareness, "higher power," and hope.

RECOVERY SERIES (1985; 50 min.)
Cost: $50.00
Available from National Film Board
(ARF Library #2090)

AUDIENCE: *Adults, health professionals, women in recovery*

SYNOPSIS: The Recovery Series is a compilation of five women's stories of their recovery. Debbie and Sharon are sisters who grew up in an alcoholic family and had alcohol problems themselves. Both are now sober and are taking a greater interest in their Native culture. Delia is a health care professional and a single parent. Even while treating others for alcohol problems, she drank heavily herself. Her friends finally persuaded her to get help herself. Although she has completed a treatment program, she is still having great difficulty, but is working part-time.

Lori, a lesbian, is interviewed about her past drinking and her treatment. She says that she drank "alcoholically" right from the start. After many years she admitted herself to a psychiatric ward. There she suffered such withdrawal effects that she realized she needed more treatment. She learned to restructure her life at a woman's treatment centre, and has been sober for five years.

Ruth had used heroin, alcohol and prescription drugs. She worked the street to pay for her habit. She had tried to get off drugs on her own and suffered severe withdrawal. Following treatment, she has learned to take care of herself and not blame others for her problems.

THE SECOND HALF: TOM HENDERSON STORY (1990; 29 min.)
Cost: $595.00
Available from Kinetic
(ARF Library # 969)

AUDIENCE: *12 years+, athletes, substance users*

SYNOPSIS: Former U.S. football pro Tom Henderson begins by telling his audience, "I am a drug addict and an alcoholic." He goes on to recount his decline from stardom as a Dallas Cowboy in the 1970s. Henderson explains, "In 1976 I met a drug that changed my life — cocaine." In 1979 he was fired from the Cowboys and bounced from team to team, then to a hospital bed before beginning his recovery from drug abuse. Game footage and comments from former teammates are included.

SICK OF STRESS (RELAXATION MODULE) (1989; 23 min.)
Cost: $395.00
Available from Kinetic
(ARF Library #11020)

Examines the cause of stress and ways of diffusing it and demonstrates techniques to manage stress and maintain positive mental attitudes.

STAYING OFF COCAINE: AVOIDING RELAPSE (1988; 38 min.)
Cost: $225.00 (US)
Available from FMS Productions
(ARF Library # 852)

AUDIENCE: *Treatment, professional training*

SYNOPSIS: Dr. Washton and recovering cocaine abusers describe how to stay off cocaine: addicts must take personal responsibility for their recovery, abstain from all drug use and change their lifestyle.

If a relapse occurs, it is important to know that this is not uncommon. Dr. Washton advises addicts to ride out the craving, learn from the experience and try again. It is necessary to deal with negative emotional states, keep busy and active, and build a new support network.

STAYING SOBER, KEEPING STRAIGHT
   (1988; 35 min.)
Cost: $670.00
Available from Kinetic
(ARF Library #880)
AUDIENCE: *Adults, health professionals, drug users*
SYNOPSIS: Several methods of avoiding relapse are illustrated through the experiences of three people who have struggled with drug dependence and overcome it. John, a recovering addict, learns he is better able to resist using if he anticipates situations in which he will be offered a drink or a drug. Mike learns that anger often triggers his desire to drink and that attending regular AA meetings can help him from slipping back into old habits. Lisa, a cocaine addict, relapses, thereby learning the hard way that she cannot use drugs and alcohol socially, and that it can be dangerous to resume relationships with friends who are still using.

THE THREE-HEADED DRAGON   (1979; 25 min.)
Cost: $450.00
Available from Kinetic
(ARF Library #460)
SYNOPSIS: Using the simile of a three-headed dragon, Chuck Brussette lectures on a theory of alcoholism that proposes that there are three major components of this disease: drinking, thinking and feeling. Resolution of the problem can occur if each of the three "heads of the dragon" is recognized as a barrier to recovery and is confronted. Speaking from personal experience, Brussette states that in order for the alcoholic to recover, he or she must (1) stop drinking completely; (2) learn how to deal with emotional immaturity and feelings of insecurity and

low self-esteem; and (3) modify his or her mode of thinking, in order to halt the process of denial and self-deception. It is only when the alcoholic has recognized and confronted all three barriers that he or she can be said to be on the way to recovery.

12 STEPS   (1986; 35 min.)
Cost: $99.00 (US)
Available from Kinetic
(ARF Library #739)
SYNOPSIS: Many people who have had problems in their lives, such as alcoholism, gambling or overeating, have found that by living the "12-Step program" they have been able to recover and live happy, productive lives. People who are using this program explain what each step means to them and how they use it in their daily lives.

VICTORY OVER ALCOHOL   (1989; 30 min.)
Cost: $285.00
Available from Kinetic
(ARF Library # 2105)
AUDIENCE: *Adults, support groups, alcoholics*
SYNOPSIS: Two professional narrators aim their presentation at all people with alcohol problems, particularly those who are just beginning their recovery. Interviews with their clients are mixed with comments and advice. The message is to deal with the alcohol first because it is stressful and often masks other emotional or personal problems. Suggestions are made as to how one can care for the whole person with nutrition, stress reduction, exercise, vitamins, support groups, and learning to socialize differently and enjoy the pleasures of life.

WALKING IN PAIN   (1988; 50 min.)
Cost: $550.00
Available from Kinetic
(ARF Library #895)
AUDIENCE: *Adults, health professionals, Natives*
SYNOPSIS: Alcoholism and drug addiction are among the most serious problems currently threatening

Native Indian people. At the Native Round Lake Treatment Centre near Armstrong, British Columbia, Marg Mackie-Orr, a senior counsellor, talks with native clients, both individually and in groups, to help them understand and overcome the root causes of their alcohol and drug abuse. She believes that drinking is a sickness of the ego and the key to recovery lies in unlocking and dealing with suppressed emotions. Alcoholics are in constant anguish, walking in the pain of self-remorse, guilt, hurt, hatred and anger.

WALL OF DENIAL   (1992; 47 min.)
Cost: $495.00
Available from Kinetic
(ARF Library #1090)
AUDIENCE: *Drug users, men in recovery, prison counsellors*
SYNOPSIS: Speaking to their peers, Otis, Roy and John explain how they became addicted, how they denied their substance abuse and related problems (in particular, crime) and how they finally sought help. Host Rick, also a recovering addict, introduces concepts such as "lying to ourselves" and "dealing with our feelings."

VENDORS

Canadian Learning Company
95 Vansittart Avenue
Woodstock ON N4S 6E3
E-mail: info@canlearn.com
Web: http://www.canlearn.com
Tel.: 519-537-1035

FMS Productions, Inc.
1029 Cindy Lane, Box 5016
Carpinteria CA 93014
Tel.: 800-421-4609

Kinetic Inc.
511 Bloor Street West, 2nd Floor
Toronto ON M5S 1Y4
E-mail: info@kineticinc.com
Web: http://www.kineticinc.com
Tel.: 416-538-6613

National Film Board of Canada
Zoom In, D5
Box 6100, Station Centre-Ville
Montreal QC H3C 3H5
Web: http://www.nfb.ca
Tel.: 514-496-2573

INTRODUCTION TO RECOVERY

Appendix B: Evaluation

APPENDIX B:

EVALUATION

It is important to evaluate how clients receive the modules. This one-page questionnaire for group participants will help you to identify the following:

1. what participants liked and disliked about the modules
2. what participants found helpful
3. what participants would like to change about the modules.

This feedback will increase your understanding of what the group meant for the participants and what is important to them.

Evaluation Tips for Facilitators

• At the end of a group, each participant should be given a pencil and the one-page questionnaire on the next page.

• Facilitators should make sure that they have the questionnaires, pencils, and envelopes organized before the session begins.

• Facilitators should ensure confidentiality by asking a participant to collect the written responses and place them in an envelope that is then sealed and given to the agency's secretary. Assure participants that their comments will be completely confidential and anonymous.

• Explain the rationale behind the age and gender questions.

Some participants may use the quick and easy way to fill out the questionnaire — providing one-word answers for each of the questions. For example:

1. What did you like about today's session?
   "Everything"
2. What did you dislike about today's session?
   "Nothing"
3. What did you find helpful about today's session?
   "Everything"
4. What changes would you like to see in this group?
   "None"

To avoid answers like these, assure participants that their comments are valuable to you, will help you to become a better presenter and will benefit other people who come to the withdrawal management centre.

Participant Evaluation Form

Date:_____   Module topic:_____

What did you like about today's group session?

What did you dislike about today's group session?

What did you find helpful about today's group session?

What changes would you like to see in this group?

What more information would you like to have added to the presentation?
What other issues would you like to discuss during group?

Your gender   Male ☐   Female ☐   Your age _____ years
(This question lets us know if this group   *(This question helps us know if this group*
helps both men and women.)   *works well for all age groups.)*

Facilitator's Evaluation Form

Evaluation of *Introduction to Recovery: A Facilitator's Guide to Effective Early Recovery Groups*

As you gain experience facilitating early recovery groups, and as you receive feedback from participants, you may become aware of other issues or develop ideas that would be helpful to other withdrawal management and early recovery groups. This information would be valuable to us and may lead to the development of additional modules that can be added to your manual in the future. We invite you to send us your comments using the following questionnaire.

Please take a few moments to answer the following questions and to write any additional comments or suggestions, and mail this form to the address provided below.

Please rate the following statements.

	strongly disagree				strongly agree
1. The guide was easy to use.					
	1	2	3	4	5
2. The information was well organized.					
	1	2	3	4	5
3. Participants responded positively to the presentations.	1	2	3	4	5

Please answer the following questions.

Did you have any problems using this guide for the presentations? If yes, please explain:

What did you like about the guide?

What improvements would you make to the guide?

What other topics would you like to have added to the guide?

What other resources would you like to have added to the guide?

When completed, please return this evaluation form to:
Marketing and Sales Services
Addiction Research Foundation Division
Centre for Addiction and Mental Health
33 Russell Street
Toronto, Ontario M5S 2S1